"Brother" AL STRICKLIN

My Years

with

Bob Wills

BOB WILLS
March 6, 1905 — May 13, 1975

My Years

with

Bob Wills

by Al Stricklin

with Jon McConal

EAKIN PRESS   ★   Burnet, Texas

---

i

Library of Congress Cataloging in Publication Data

Stricklin, Al, 1908—
    My years with Bob Wills.

    1. Stricklin, Al, 1908-   2. Wills, Bob, 1905-1975.   3. Country
musicians—Correspondence, Reminiscences, etc. I. McConal, Jon,
1937-joint author. II. Title.
ML 417.S92A3   785'.092'4 [B]   76-7228
ISBN 0-89015-240-3

First Edition, April 1976
Second Printing, May 1976
Second Edition, 1980

ii

"BROTHER" AL STRICKLIN

iii

Dedicated

to my dear friends

Smokey Dacus, Joe Frank Ferguson,

and Leon McAuliffe and the rest of the

Texas Playboys

Foreword

Alton Meeks Stricklin was born on January 29, 1908, in the tiny but lively settlement of Antioch, which today is nothing but a memory in southern Johnson County, Texas. Al, as he later became known, was the son of Zebedee Meeks Stricklin, a tall, lean, hardworking man, and Annie Benton, whose parents were one of the pioneer families of Antioch.

Al was the youngest of the couple's three children. He displayed an early interest in music. His father was a good breakdown fiddle player and Al learned to play chords on the piano to accompany his daddy on the fiddle.

When Al was five, his older sister, Violet, began to show him some simple tunes on the piano. He soon picked up other melodies and added accompaniment. By the time he was twelve, he could play many of the popular songs.

But these songs were considered "jazz," and the deeply religious people of the community thought jazz was sinful. Local preachers spent many hours condemning such music because it was played in dance halls where dancing was done. And, dancing was almost as bad as stealing horses.

So Al confined his music to the more acceptable folk songs or sacred music. But, Meeks began to secretly encourage his son to play the music he liked best and hoped for a day when it would become more acceptable and perhaps profitable.

Al finished high school in Grandview, Texas. He worked his way through college by playing for school functions and teaching piano. He taught students to play by ear and to improvise and play good full chords with rhythm. He got many offers to play for dances during his college years, but he was fearful at first. He still remembered the stern admonitions from the preachers.

Al Stricklin had to leave school when he was twenty-two because of the great stock market crash. He came home to try to help his family survive. The family grew all of their own food. During this bleak period, people forgot that dance music was sinful. So Al began to pick up a few dollars playing for dances.

He was working for KFJZ in Fort Worth when he first met Bob Wills, who later was to play a powerful role in Stricklin's life. But, before that was to happen, Stricklin lost his job at the radio station in 1933. He and his brother Benton returned to the family farm in order to have a place to eat and sleep.

Al got a job as a teacher making $90.00 a month. Benton was making $12.50 a week working at a bank. In 1935 Al again got a job at KFJZ playing daily programs with the "Hi-Fliers." That was where he was when Bob Wills walked back into his life and offered him a job. Stricklin took it. This is the story of his experiences with Bob Wills as one of the Texas Playboys.

BOB WILLS and his TEXAS PLAYBOYS.

Acknowledgments

Bob Wills had several unhappy marriages before Betty Anderson became his wife in 1942. Then, for more than thirty-two years, especially the last years of his life, she loved him when a lot of other people didn't, or wouldn't admit that they did. I wish to express my appreciation to Betty for giving me many hours of her time in helping with background material for my book, and for her friendship.

I want to thank Merle Haggard, who was the one that got the old gang of original Texas Playboys, and Bob Wills, together again in September 1971. It was during this reunion that the notion to write this book struck me. Merle told me he thought it was a great idea and his urging helped me to do it.

I must thank Jon McConal of the *Fort Worth Star-Telegram*. I hammered out a manuscript and Jon put a great deal of time and effort into helping me make it into a book. Since musicians do not always act like choirboys, there are some stories in the book that are a little on the earthy side. I tell my friends and relatives that Jon put those bad words in there, but he tells his mother that I did. I hope no one is offended by my choice of stories or by the "bite" that somehow got into the language that describes them.

I want to thank my wife, Betty, my daughters, Nancy and Judy, and my son, David—these loved ones who helped and encouraged me over the rough spots in composing and the times when it all looked pretty hopeless. Nancy did a great service typing my manuscript.

I offer a special thanks for all the many ex-Texas Playboys everywhere, deceased and alive, and particularly the ones I worked with personally.

Many thanks go to the new breed of musicians like Alvin Crow, Red Steagall, Ray Benson of Asleep at the Wheel and the "Wheel's" former piano player Jim Haber ("Floyd Domino"), and the not-so-new breed like Waylon Jennings and Willie Nelson, who have had such a large part in keeping Western swing alive.

Deep appreciation and affection go to the many faithful Texas Playboy fans, from my own generation to my grand-children's. It's these people who make the Bob Wills story a legend and it's for them that I wrote this book.

My humble gratitude goes to Ed Eakin of Burnet, Texas, whose patience, enthusiasm, and integrity have made possible the telling of my story.

A. S.
Cleburne, Texas
February 1980

Contents

AL STRICKLIN

Prologue

IT WAS MIDAFTERNOON and the sun was shining and I knew somewhere not too far from where I was standing there were waving fields of wheat and oats being nudged by the wind and sun along their road to being ripe and ready for harvest. I knew that sooner or later them old combines would be firing up and the noisy chug-chug-chug-alugging of their engines would be sputtering and they would be belching black smoke into the air and the men on top of them would be clanking their levers and gears and be heading out to the fields. And I knew that they'd get there and then they'd drop their power lifts and turn on the power takeoffs and the big sickles on the combine would begin their loud and steady click-click-clicking and the blades would start snipping them golden heads off and start sending them up the conveyor belts where they'd be belched into the bowels of the big combines, down there where all of them gears and cogs would be turning and clanking and ripping the wheat from the heads and then barreling it on up into them big old bins and the chaff and dust would spiral up into the air and make the combine drivers itch and wish it would hurry up and be quitting time. I knew that would happen soon. Because

1

harvest time was coming. You could smell it in the Oklahoma sunshine.

But, I wasn't there at Tulsa, Oklahoma, standing on the grounds of the Eastwood Baptist Church in a suit that fit me a little too tight and made me feel a little too hot, waiting for the harvest. I was there to attend the funeral of a man whose magic as a musician made a harvest in the field of music that is still being felt and talked about. That man was the great Bob Wills, a man whom I learned not only to respect deeply as a musician, but love as a man. You see, Bob Wills plucked me out of the sparse fields of the depression when my wife and I were having to beg soup bones from the butcher shop in order to survive. He planted me in his band, and for some seven years I harvested part of the glory that Bob reaped with his music.

I was his piano player.

That was many years ago. But that day in Tulsa they were as vivid in my mind as a kid getting his first big mouth of bubble gum.

I kept telling myself that "Bob was dead — Bob was dead." But the memories wouldn't go away. And, I kept thinking, if death is appropriate and I know it is, then Bob's funeral at Tulsa was also appropriate. That's the way he had always wanted it. The Moores' Funeral Home of Tulsa had buried Bob's parents and long before he died he had said that he wanted the Moores to bury him.

So here we all were at Tulsa at the Eastwood Baptist Church waiting for the funeral to begin. I thought it was fitting that Bob's last rites would be at a Baptist Church. Because Bob actually was a Baptist. He probably hadn't been inside a church for fifty years but he had a religion of his own that all of us Playboys knew about.

He had his own way of getting near God. It was that close kind of feeling. Bob always thought it should be a personal thing between a man and God. And, I think that he always wished that he had gone on and become a preacher instead of a performer. I can remember many times his

2

saying that he felt like he ought to be out there working for God instead of the devil.

He would get a feeling of loneliness and sorrow and he'd say, "Al, I ought to get out of this dancing. I ought to get out and start preaching again."

He displayed that feeling in many ways. I remember once when we were playing a big New Year's Eve dance and everybody was drunk and having a good time and hollering and raising hell and there must have been several thousand of them when all of a sudden Bob just up and raises his hands and says, "May I have your attention please."

Everybody shut up quick, because Bob always had control over the crowd. Then he said, "Let's don't ever forget the Man upstairs who is letting us have this good time. Let's get serious. As a matter of fact, I think we ought to sing a religious song."

And we did. Bob pointed his fiddle bow at me and I hit an F chord and Bob started singing, "What a Friend We Have in Jesus." Before two lines had passed, all of them drunks were singing. That was Bob's religion.

He also showed his faith by playing for funerals. That would happen two or three times a week. We'd go to the sticks or we'd go to the big cities and play funerals. It didn't make any difference. Somebody would call and say, "Bob, my Mama's died and one of her last requests was that you come and play at her funeral." And Bob and us Playboys would go and we'd play. For nothing.

When we'd start back home, Bob would get real sentimental. He'd be sad. He'd say, "Boys, that could be one of us." And today it was. It was Bob. . . .

The crowd was already big. And more were arriving by the second. Old pickups, beat up Chevys and sleek and shiny Buicks, Oldsmobiles and Cadillacs were driving up. People dressed in suits that had twenty-year-old creases in them and people dressed in $500 silk rigs were coming into the church. I heard one of them saying, "Isn't it fitting that they're burying old Bob here . . . right here in Tulsa."

3

Right there in Tulsa, I was thinking. Right there where Bob got it all to going, really. The town that caused us to write one of his most famous songs, "Take Me Back to Tulsa." Aw, what a time that was.

I got to thinking how that song came about. Back in the '30s when we were going on the road so much and we'd be tired and want to get back home, we'd pile in our old bus and somehow the saying got started, "Take me back to Tulsa." Then we went to Chicago in 1936 for a pretty big deal and stayed there several days and before long the boys were kinda humming, "Take me back to Tulsa." That's when Bob and Tommy Duncan decided to make up a song to that title and it was "Take Me Back to Tulsa."

All of a sudden my thoughts were interrupted by someone whispering, "There's the senator. There's the senator." And it was. Senator McFaddin of Oklahoma came in all dressed up. He was going to give the eulogy. Right after he sat down, the funeral started.

Johnny Gimble and Keith Coleman, two of the original Playboys, and Curley Lewis were playing the fiddle up there where the choir generally was in the church. Eldon Shamblin was playing the standard guitar. They played real soft and gentle and the senator began reading the eulogy.

They played "Faded Love," "What a Friend We Have in Jesus," "Farther Along," "Maiden's Prayer," and "Betty's Waltz." You could hear the rustle of handkerchiefs as people dabbed at their eyes and music just gently filled the auditorium, seeking out the dark corners and blending in with the sunshine that was streaming in the windows.

The senator had finished the eulogy and all of a sudden it began. Bob's most famous song. The song that had sold as many records as any in history, topped only by "White Christmas." Bob's song. "San Antonio Rose." As the players got into it, they started rolling the casket back to the foyer. That's the first time that Betty Wills, Bob's beautiful and devoted wife, displayed emotion. She said, "Oh, no." They

4

caught her and supported her and all of us old Playboys began wiping our eyes. We knew it was ending.

They opened the casket back in the foyer and it must have taken thirty minutes for all of the people to pass by and view the body. I didn't want to look at him, but I did. He didn't look like Bob Wills. He looked so artificial. All patched up. All painted up. Hands gnarled up. So skinny. The last few years had left him that way. The stroke. The year of a coma in a hospital in Fort Worth, Texas. No, this wasn't Bob Wills.

Later, they fed us. All of the old original Playboys. There were several hundred other people. They all came up and shook our hands and practically every one of them had some old story about Bob.

As we were standing there eating and talking, this lanky fellow walked up. He grinned and stuck out his hand, and he said, "Al, bet you don't know me."

I grinned back. I remembered. I said, "Yeah, I remember you. How could I forget? You are Herman Arnspiger."

I hadn't seen him since 1942. He hadn't changed much. He was still erect and tall. He played the guitar for Bob way back. He used to hold his guitar up into the microphone to get some sound since he didn't have any amplifier.

"Yeah, I remember, Herman. I'll never forget. It was 1931," I said. It was a long time ago. The first time I ever met Bob Wills. But, out of that meeting grew memories that funerals would never kill. They are like a big wheat harvest. Full of golden kernels of wheat. A farmer never forgets when he plunges his hands into that first big bin of wheat. He's like me. I'll never forget those years with Bob Wills. He was the greatest.

Chapter 1

THERE ARE MANY DAYS that I'll never forget. Certainly I'll never forget that day of Bob Wills' funeral. But there are several others that anchor large portions of poignancy in my mind. One was September 27, 1971. It was one of the most eventful days in my life. It is among my greatest memories — as touching as the day I kissed my first girl or the day I got my high school diploma or the day I married.

All of those days were special because I guess you could say they meant that some of my dreams came true. That's the way it is with September 27, 1971. A dream-came-true day. And it inspired me to write this book.

On that beautiful fall day in sun-splashed California in a magnificent home about twelve miles from Bakersfield, Bob Wills, and ten of his former Texas Playboys, including myself, got together.

Bob was in an almost helpless condition then, his lanky body rendered almost helpless by the ravages of a series of strokes. But, he was there. And many of the Texas Playboys who were there had not seen each other for more than thirty years.

I don't know when I've had more fun and pleasure than that day. You know how memories are. Particularly memories of yesterday that are polished more perfectly with the passage of time. And we were swapping some memories that day.

Merle Haggard, the famed country and western singer, who I think is the greatest going today, had made the event possible. As a boy and a young man he had made every effort to see and hear Bob Wills and His Texas Playboys. And, a few years ago, to show his dedication to Bob, Haggard had recorded an album and dedicated it to Bob. He named it simple. It was, "To the Best Damn Fiddle Player in the World."

The album was successful. That's when Merle decided to have Bob and some of his old gang come out to his home near Bakersfield and play and make some tapes for perhaps another album.

Besides myself and Bob, there were Leon McAuliffe, Eldon Shamblin, Smokey Dacus, Johnnie Lee Wills, Luke Wills, Joe Holley, Alex Brashear, Johnny Gimble, Tiny Moore and Glenn Duncan.

So there we sat all together, working just like old times and swapping stories during breaks. But there was something missing. That was the old master. The man who started it all; the man who could get 110 percent effort out of his musicians like a good football coach; the man who was feared and loved by his men; the man who could sell his product like nobody else, as testified to by the thousands of people who turned out to listen, even during blizzard-like conditions sometimes; the man . . . Bob Wills. He was not playing with us.

He sat helplessly in his wheelchair. His brown eyes, still as keen and piercing — like a sharp jackknife — as they ever were, kept watching each one of us. He would nod his approval and encouragement and every once in a while he would give that wink at you that always brought forth that extra 10 percent from his musicians.

It was hard for me to hold my feelings inside. Because I knew how much he wanted to be up there with us. I knew how he must have been hurting inside for not being able to get up there with us and point his fiddle bow at Leon and say, "Take it away, Leon," and then let out that shrill yell of "Ahh-Ha!" that became as popular among his Texas fans as the battle cry of the Texas pioneers, "Remember the Alamo!" I knew how he wanted to say during the time it came for a break on the piano, "Here's Al Stricklin, now. You old piano pounder."

But, we kept playing. Merle did some vocals and some fiddle numbers. And, Merle's wife, Bonnie Owens, a talented entertainer, also did some vocals.

I kept thinking as I sat there playing with all those familiar faces, some of them weathered considerably by time, that something should be done. And, before the session ended after about nine hours of playing, the decision hit me of what I must do.

The urge became very strong. Before I left, I had a talk with Merle about it. I said that so many people had enjoyed Bob Wills and His Texas Playboys that something ought to be done about it. Merle thought my idea was a good one.

He loved hearing some of the inside story of the Playboys during their great years in the 1930s. He also thought that the most interesting period in the life and career of Bob Wills and His Playboys was the years from 1931 until the beginning of World War II.

I was glad that Merle thought my idea a good one. Because it is my belief that real life can be as interesting, if not more so, than fiction. I feel that my years with Bob Wills were kinda like fiction in many ways. That's why I think that the idea that kinda bubbled up from my piano keyboard that day at Haggard's is a good one. I want to tell you the story of my years with Bob Wills . . . the old master who wrote a page of history in the music field that will never be forgotten.

Chapter 2

I WAS THE STAFF pianist at KFJZ Radio Station in Fort Worth, Texas when Bob Wills walked into my life. I also was chief collector of bad accounts in advertising. And I was one of the worst at that. I was just too good at listening to hard luck stories because there were a lot of them during that period.

I had been playing some dances. I played what I called jazz. But anything with a beat then was considered jazz. Really, it was more pop than anything, according to today's standards. The bands I played with did things like "Five Feet Two," "Dinah," "Nobody's Sweetheart Now," and "Darkness on the Delta." Things like that went good with the crowds. We called our band the "Unholy Three." Another group I played with was called "Tune Tinkers."

At that time the only fiddle music I'd heard was some breakdown stuff. My dad played that. But I wasn't too much impressed by fiddle music. I'll have to admit Bob Wills changed all of that.

I was lolling around the studio that day waiting for my time to go on the air when I heard a small commotion in the small reception room. Opal Copeland, our receptionist, was confronted by three men wanting an audition at the

THE FIRST COMPLETE band Bob Wills had after World War II. This photo of Bob Wills and His Texas Playboys was taken in the Los Angeles area in 1945. People known personally by Al Stricklin are: Laura Lee McBride (first girl singer); Joe Holly (fiddler on the left); Louis Tierney (fiddler next to Joe); Bob (near mike); Billie Jack Wills (drums); Rip Ramsey (bass); Millard Kelso (piano); Tommy Duncan (vocalist on far right).

"THE UNHOLY THREE" at Radio Station KFJZ, Fort Worth, Texas in 1931. Left to right are Doug Blair, Larry White and Al Stricklin.

station. Opal talked to Max Shippe, our station manager, and he said "Sure, we give auditions to anyone."

Since our program director was on vacation, it was my duty to take the three men into the studio and set up for the audition. They looked like bad hombres. All needed shaves and Bob had his fiddle in a flour sack. I later learned that he had hocked it earlier for $5 and had borrowed it out of hock for this audition.

I introduced myself to them and they seemed nice. I learned that Wills would be playing the fiddle, Herman Arnspiger would be seconding on the guitar and Milton Brown would be the main vocalist.

"Boys, what kind of music do you play?" I asked.

"Different," said Wills. "The Wills Fiddle Band plays different."

Was it ever different. I adjusted the mike and turned the switch so we could listen in the outer room. The Wills Fiddle Band went to it.

I'd never heard anything like it. They cut loose on a song called, "Who Broke the Lock on the Henhouse Door?" Milton sang with great gusto and Bob swung his fiddle wildly up and down, and all of the time just playing the hell out of it. Arnspiger was whacking and twirling and and plunking his guitar like it was a piece of fire and he wanted to let it go but couldn't.

I thought at first they were making fun of some kind of comedy song. But then they went into "Four or Five Times" and "The Craw Dad Song" and I realized that they were playing with feeling. Straight from the heart.

As I learned later, Bob Wills never made fun of any song and he always put the same feeling into every song he ever did. But that day, I'll admit, those guys had me in stitches.

You must understand that this was really strange music to a guy like me who had worked so hard for so many years to try to master jazz on the piano. I thought that their type of thing would have been perfect for a Medicine Show.

10

There were hundreds of them in the country during those times.

They were often the only organized entertainment that the small towns had. A sharpie who claimed he was a doctor would show up at a town in an old Model T and set up a small stage and go to selling colored water, claiming that it was some powerful tonic that would cure you of anything from hemorrhoids to ingrown toenails.

I later found out that Bob Wills had indeed played in one of the medicine shows. They would introduce him as "Rastus," and he would come out and play his fiddle while the sharpie was selling the tonic.

After the Wills Fiddle Band got through that day, I asked them if they would like to be put on again. "We sure would," said Bob.

I guess we did that for a couple of reasons. One was that they did entertain us. But another was that during those days we didn't have any disc jockeys or turntables and we were looking for talent all of the time. So we gave them a chance. Were we in for a surprise.

They received more fan mail than all the rest of the station's entertainers put together. The post office called and said it had more mail than it could carry and that we would have to send someone down there to pick up the cards and letters. There were several hundred. The Wills Fiddle Band was hired for $15 a week. They played six days a week. To guys who hadn't eaten regularly, that was good money.

After they left KFJZ, I didn't really pay much attention to Bob Wills and his band. Matter of fact, I don't think I really cared about them. But, I was like a lot of "legit" musicians at that time. And, that was one reason that Bob's music was so slow to be recognized by the music profession.

Those were the days of the big bands — Paul Whiteman, The Dorseys, Glenn Miller, Ted Lewis, Casa Loma and others. The singers of the day were people like Bing Crosby, Kate Smith, Eddie Cantor, Nick Lucas and Louis

11

Armstrong. Can you possibly imagine then, what impact "Who Broke the Lock on the Henhouse Door?" had on people like me who had never heard anything like it? The only entertainer who was doing anything near that was a young guitar playing singer. His name was Jimmy Rogers.

Anyway, I didn't pay much attention to Bob Wills after he left KFJZ. I vaguely remember hearing that he had hooked onto a program at Waco in 1933. He played there with a radio station. His band was just called "The Playboys."

During that time, I had started teaching school at a small place in Johnson County known as Island Grove. I taught and played a job now and then. If I got $5 a night, I thought that was great. I also was teaching piano to a few students.

In the summer of 1935, I got on with a band called "The High Fliers." It was a studio band at KFJZ. We worked on commission. We would play three shows a day. And each time we would change our name. To get a different sound, we would trade instruments.

About fall of that year, I signed a contract at the school. I also was playing in a band at a place called "The Cinderella Roof," over on South Jennings in Fort Worth. I was getting $5 for Saturday night and $3 for Wednesday night.

It was on a Saturday night that Bob Wills walked into my life again. We were in the middle of a dance and in he came. He was wearing expensive cowboy boots. He had on an expensive and tailored western suit. His pants were tucked inside his boots and he was wearing spurs. He had on a little black tie with a large diamond stickpin in it. And had on a big white western hat. He was tall and straight. He walked up to me and said, "Hi, Mr. Stricklin."

"Are you Bob Wills?" I asked.

He kinda grinned and said he was. I was impressed. And, shocked. He didn't look like the Bob Wills I had

12

known who had played "Who Broke the Lock on the Henhouse Door?" those three years ago.

He said he wanted to talk to me when I got a break. So when we finished, Bob and I sat down in a booth. He said, "Strick, I've hit it pretty big up in Tulsa. I've got a radio program and it's going pretty good. We're making about $2000 a week."

I nearly swallowed my Adam's apple. Wills continued: "I got an old boy who sings. His name is Tommy Duncan. He also plays the piano, but he doesn't know too much about it. He gets a lot of laughs but I'm looking for a better piano player. I'm going to need one in September."

"Are you offering me a job?" I asked.

"Yeah, I am," he said.

"How much does it pay?" I asked.

"Thirty bucks," said Wills.

"A month?" I asked.

"No, a week," he replied.

There went my Adam's apple again.

Well, I knew that it was good money. But something else that happened shortly after Bob walked into the dance hall had made me sit up and take notice. That was the way the crowd had reacted to him. Much to my surprise, they knew him from his fame in Oklahoma. That, plus Bob's way of just charming people, had turned the crowd on.

We had asked him to play some with us as soon as we learned he was there. He obliged. He borrowed Pat Trotter's fiddle and took off on "Don't let the Deal Go Down." Suddenly the crowd forgot about dancing. They were crowding around Wills. Who wanted to dance when they could get a close-up of the "Best Damn Fiddle Player in the World"? Right then, I got a preview of what it would be like to be a member of Bob's band.

So here we sat talking about me going to work for him. He had a way of making you feel confident and capable.

13

Before I knew it, I was beginning to think that I was pretty damn good myself.

He began talking again about why he wanted me.

"Now, old Tommy knows a few chords and he's been doing his stuff at the dances. But we are going to make some recordings in September and we need a piano player who can play some breaks and chords that will be acceptable to the recording people," he said.

Bob eyed the milling crowd, many of whom were coming over and shaking his hand and saying they knew him back when. Then he continued, "Strick, we work hard. We travel a lot and we don't get much sleep. It's hotter than hell at a lot of the places where we play. You can just smell them old bodies getting all lathered up and emotional. And then there's the winters. They're just as bad as the summer. Your fingers are going to get cold, and when you hit them old keys they are going to hurt, but you've got to keep smiling. And, keep playing."

Someone else walked up and interrupted with a long story about a grandfather who played the fiddle only on Tuesdays because he was afraid that the Lord would strike him dead if he played on Saturdays and got people in such a good mood they would go and party themselves out and not want to go to church on Sunday, and his grandpa sure as hell wasn't going to play on Sundays for fear of what the Lord might think about that, so he only played on Tuesdays.

"But he sounds just like you," said the man.

Bob winked at me and shook the man's hand and he left and then Bob continued, "But, Strick, it has its rewards. The boys are all friendly and cooperative and work well together. And the crowds . . . well, Strick, they'll turn you on. They've got enthusiasm. They'll like you."

Some more people came up and interrupted again and I didn't really know what they were saying. I was stunned, like someone had hit me in the head with a two-by-four. Finally, the people left, and Bob continued, "Kid, as I said,

14

if you want to come to work for me, I will start you at $30. And every ninety days we will give you a five dollar per week raise until you get up to $50 per week."

He laughed then, and said, "What do you say, man?"

Of course, I couldn't imagine anybody making that kind of money, especially doing something they enjoyed. It took me a time to find my voice. When I did, I said, "This is the greatest thing that ever happened to me. I want to talk it over with my wife."

He stayed the rest of the evening and I must admit that I probably didn't do too good a job of playing the rest of that time. But, before he left, I told him, "Bob, I'm sure that I'll be there. It's just a matter of me telling my wife."

"I'm glad to hear that, Strick. We need you and want you. I will be looking for you."

When I got home that night my wife was still awake. I told her about the offer. She was elated. There were several reasons for that. Number one, she knew how much I enjoyed playing and she knew that playing with Bob Wills would really be an exciting chance for me. But there was another reason of equal importance.

Times were very lean then. By that, I mean people were looking like old hound dogs that had been chasing coons for a month without anything to eat. Take my wife and me.

We made our budget. We payed for the things like rent, utilities, car expenses and other necessities. What we had left, we spent for groceries. Lots of times we would be entirely out of money several days before I got my next pay check. We might have some beans and water gravy. Sometimes she would ask the butcher for a soup bone to give the dog.

We didn't have a dog. But the bone, we hoped, would still have a little meat left on it so that we could make a little soup from it to give us strength.

So actually, my wife didn't just say that it was a good idea to take the job. She started shouting. For joy.

15

"When can we go, honey?" she shouted. Then for good measure, she added, "Hallelujah!"

I got a letter off to Bob that next day. I told him that I was anxious to go to work for him and would he verify by return mail and tell me when and where to report for work. I still have that letter. It says:

Dear Alton:

This will acknowledge receipt of your letter of August 23 in which you state that you are interested in joining with me in my organization.

I have recently organized another band. However, this band is going under the name of my father, as Young John and His Lone Star Rangers, broadcasting over KVOO from 6:30 until 7:00 o'clock in the morning. This program is featuring my dad in old-time fiddling. However we have another feature that we use in playing the more popular numbers on the radio and dance engagements.

There are eight in this band. I would like to use you in my band, but I don't know whether I could place you in it just now or not. But, if you will come up here and go to work with the recently organized band, I will guarantee you thirty dollars ($30.00) a week.

I have recently signed a contract to make some Brunswick recordings, and I would like to use you in my band in making these recordings. Now the band that I would like for you to go to work in is going to be all right. I am rehearsing them myself and there is a chance that their program will go commercial in a very few days. So regardless of where I might use you, I will pay you the $30.00 per week. If you are interested in this proposition, you may make your arrangements and come ahead as soon as you can.

16

I am making these recordings sometime between September 15 and September 30. Thank you for your inquiry and your willingness to join me and my organization.

Actually, we didn't get that letter for a week. And while we were waiting, I started wondering if Bob had been really serious about me coming to play for him, or maybe he was just drunk and didn't know what he had said.

Then when I got the letter, I felt like maybe he had changed his mind about my playing and was sort of passing it off by putting me in his dad's band. I almost backed out because of that. I had had previous experience of playing in newly organized bands that supposedly were going to be great. They flopped by the dozens. For every 1000 of those kind there would be about one that actually made it good.

Had I known Bob then as I later got to know him, I would have known that his offer was genuine. He never let anybody down in his life. And later I found out what caused him to express some of the uncertainties in his letter.

When he had first started talking to the other guys in his band about me, and had told them that I was a college man and a schoolteacher, they all thought that I might be a stuffed shirt, smart alec or a know-it-all. Bob also dreaded taking Tommy off the piano.

Tommy was having a ball performing on the piano and had a huge number of fans who thought that he was the greatest. I found out later that there was the possibility that Tommy might have a great resentment about losing the piano to me.

But, some of the boys knew the necessity of correct chords and melodies for the record session. They argued in my favor. They finally agreed that if I turned out to be a regular fellow or a nice humble guy who showed the proper attitude, then I would play with Bob's outfit. Of course, I didn't know all of that when my wife and I were floundering around trying to make the decision.

But, we finally decided to take the chance. I called the school board president and told him that I was leaving.

"Where are you going?" he asked.

"I'm going to play with Bob Wills," I said.

"Bob Wills who?" he asked.

He never had heard of Bob Wills. That didn't make me feel too good. I told him I was sorry that I was leaving and hoped it didn't leave him in too much of a bind.

"Naw, it sure won't do that. We've got a couple dozen applications for your job already," he said.

That statement showed how hard times were.

Well, the decision was made. We packed everything we had into our old '31 Chevy. It started about half of the time. It used oil. It coughed and sputtered when you got it in too much of a bind. It could get into a bind on level ground.

We were scared to death. We only had $20. That was our entire fortune. As we wound our way to Tulsa, we kept looking at the old sand kicking up out in the fields. It wasn't a very optimistic sight. We got there late at night and I rented us a room in the cheapest motel I could find. I still wasn't sure I had a job. Neither one of us slept very soundly that night. It was a long ways back to Texas.

Chapter 3

O N SEPTEMBER 6, just twenty-two days after Will
Rogers had been killed in an airplane crash, one of
the most historic things that ever happened to me,
happened. My wife and I got up early that morning. We
might as well have. We couldn't sleep. We didn't even
eat breakfast. We started trying to find Bob Wills and His
Texas Playboys.

I finally stopped at a service station and got some gas
and I asked this guy running the place if he knew who
Bob Wills was. He looked kinda funny and said, "Fella,
are you dopey or crazy? There ain't nobody that don't know
who Bob Wills is."

So I asked him how I could find him. He shot a big
stream of snuff juice down to the dusty ground and said,
"Well you hook a couple of rights and lefts and find your
way downtown and go to the Barrel Food Palace. That's
where he'll be."

I started to leave and he stopped me, hollering, "You'd
better take up some slack in gettin' there 'cause there's
gonna be a crowd, I'll promise you."

We found out his warning was good advice. By the
time we got down to the Barrel Food Palace, which was

19

THE TEXAS PLAYBOYS at the Blue Moon Open Air dance pavilion in Tulsa, 1939.

BOB WILLS and his Texas Playboys.

a big supermarket, my wife and I thought half of Tulsa must have been there.

"Maybe they've had an earthquake," I told her. They hadn't. It was just the crowd that turned out to hear Bob and his Playboys on their noon broadcast from the big old, sprawling supermarket.

My wife was afraid to try to work her way through the crowd. I was too. But I figured I had to. After all, I had a job with Bob Wills. At least I had a letter that said I had a job with Bob Wills. And I could quote you that letter by heart at that time.

I had never seen so many people in my life. They were jammed together like human sardines. They all were stomping their feet and grinning and chewing tobacco and dipping snuff and smoking roll-your-owns and just seemed to be in big preparation for a big event.

It took me twenty minutes to work my way inside. I only got within a hundred feet of the platform or stage or whatever you want to call it. It was made from bridge timbers that had cracks in them. I could see an old piano sitting way off in the back. The band had already started broadcasting.

I don't know why, but suddenly in the middle of a number, Bob looked out and spotted me in the crowd. He said, "Hold it boys, look who I see in that crowd. It's old Al (Nobody had ever called me Al before.) Stricklin. Let him through friends."

Two things impressed me about that. I had never been called Al before. The other thing was the way that Bob had that crowd eating out of his hand. I have never seen any other person who could hold a crowd of people spellbound the way he could. He had complete control of them. All of the time. It was always that way.

I finally made my way up to the bandstand. The crowd, after Bob's instructions, parted like a giant plow had busted open some new ground after spring rains. When I crawled up on the stand, they started applauding. I had never heard anything like that.

I also had never had an introduction like that Bob gave me. He spent nearly two minutes citing my attributes. He said, "This old Al Stricklin is a great musician. I am so fortunate to have persuaded him to give up all of that glory he was reaping down in Texas and come up here and play with me. He's a start in me building my band into greatness. Old Al Stricklin and the Texas Playboys are going to be somebody that you people of Oklahoma will be proud of."

The crowd began shouting and chanting.

"Turn him loose, Bob. Let him go, Bob."

Never had I been so flattered and built up. My ego was just like that of an old toad's that's just gorged himself on some big old fat flies in the garden dew early in the morning. I was thinking, "Man, where have I been all of my life?"

Bob kept going on with the introduction. And I kept thinking, "If he ever lets me get at that piano, I'll tear it up." And finally he said —

"Now, my good friends, I want you to hear the greatest piano player you ever heard."

He turned to me, and with that big grin of his, he said, "Tear it up, Al Stricklin."

I was as high as a kite that a kid has put extra strings on and reached the bottoms of some clouds on a summer day. I was going to tear that piano up. But, I couldn't. Tommy Duncan already had. A good third of the hammers were off. Many of the strings were broken. The tuning was so bad that I could barely make one chord, much less a run or a melody. I felt like the guy with the rope around his neck waiting to fall through that trap door. But I couldn't back out now. So I just played. Rather I played at playing.

The few notes that I did play, I couldn't hear myself. The other boys were playing their hearts out as always. But they were so loud that I figured I might as well be

21

surrounded by a bunch of African jungle drums or maybe Indian tom-toms, as this was Oklahoma.

Really, all I could do was bust them with all I had and act like I was really playing something while Bob was up there selling me with all he had. I could have won an Oscar for that performance. Not for my playing. But for my acting. I was acting like a son of a gun. I was playing nothing.

But, all of the time, Bob was dancing around and swinging his fiddle and pointing with his bow and talking and coming out with his "ahh-has" and the crowd was loving it. When we got through (and before we did, I thought I was literally finished with Bob Wills and I hadn't even completed one number), the applause was deafening. You would have thought that the president of the United States had just made a speech.

I had mixed emotions.

I thought that when Bob realized that I hadn't really done anything but beat the air, he would ship me right out of Tulsa and back to Texas. I started kinda feeling in my pocket and doing some mathematical calculations to determine how much of that $20 I had left. I figured it might get me back to Texas. But I remembered that word of the school board president who had said that there were two dozen applications for my job. So I wondered if that butcher had any good, fat soup bones on hand.

But what really had happened was that Bob knew my problems and he was covering it up and selling me to these people in Oklahoma despite the obstacles. He was convincing these good Oklahoma people that I was good and that I was playing good because Bob Wills had told them so. I learned later that Bob could sell horse manure to the pastor of the biggest church in town, if he believed in the horse.

When the radio program was over, I still was a little shaky. Then I had another first experience. When we started crawling off of the stage, dozens of people were

22

lined up to get my autograph. That had never happened to me before. I couldn't believe it was happening that day. But, I was signing my name like crazy, and I guess I finally became aware of what I was doing when I heard an old woman, saying to her friend, "Lookie, here, now, I got that nice Al Stricklin's autograph."

I was still apprehensive. Even after signing my name a couple of hundred times. I still thought that I was no good, and Bob was going to fire me.

It must have taken me an hour to get back to the car where my wife was. She was very hot, as the temperature had nudged up into the 90s.

"How did it go?" she asked.

"Badly, I'm afraid," I said.

"Well, if it went badly, I'm glad it didn't go goodly," she replied. "If it had gone goodly, I don't think you'd ever have made it back to the car."

I tried to laugh. But I couldn't. I was still scared to death.

Bob had told me that we were going to have a meeting that afternoon and rehearse. So my wife and I killed time driving around while waiting for that rehearsal. I still kept thinking I was fired. I had counted and recounted our money and knew that I had $14.75. I figured if the old Chevy didn't get too cantankerous that it would get us back to Texas. I didn't know what we'd do if we got back.

But, finally came the time for rehearsal at Uncle John's house. We called Bob's parents Uncle John and Aunt Emmy and that was where we were going to rehearse. Despite my apprehensions, my wife and I were on time.

I found me a chair inside and sat down and hung my head. I had a good worry on. I just knew that Bob was going to tell me he was disappointed in my ability and to just go on back to Texas.

He came in and saw me and he immediately came over to my chair. He put his arm around me and said, "Al, I want to apologize for that old piano at the broadcast. I know it was impossible to play and I want you to know

CROWDS GATHER to hear the Playboys at the Enid, Oklahoma Fair, 1936.

ADVERTISING "TEXAS PLAYBOY FLOUR" at the Enid, Oklahoma Fair, 1936.

that I think you are great and we are really glad to have you."

He squeezed my shoulders and continued, "Al, I'm promising you. That piano will be repaired or replaced by tomorrow."

I'll never forget the feeling that came over me after that. More than thirty-seven years later I can still feel it. That man had magic. He could turn you on and make you want to perform the impossible. I knew from then on that I could play any piano that was set in front of me. Whether it had 900 keys or just three keys. I was Bob Wills' piano player. And, I was a good one. Because that's what he said.

Chapter 4

IT DIDN'T TAKE long for me to learn about the musical magic of Bob Wills. I learned that first night after that first rehearsal. It was at a place called Glen Oak, a frame building dance hall about fifteen miles east of Bartlesville, Oklahoma.

At that time I was the only member of the band with a college education. That had really been a minus in my hiring, I later learned. Bob was afraid that I might be one of those well-educated smart alecs who was always showing off by quoting his learning and beating the other members over the head with his bat of knowledge.

So on that first trip the other band members really gave me a test. Actually, that test went on for several weeks before the guys as well as Bob decided that I was just old Al Stricklin and wore dirty socks and sometimes didn't shine my shoes and broke wind that I knew didn't smell any better than anyone else's.

The members in the band at that time were Bob Wills, fiddle and leader; Jesse Ashlock, fiddle and vocals; Art Haines, fiddle and trombone; Leon McAuliffe, steel guitar and vocals; Sleepy Johnson, guitar; Herman Arnspiger, guitar; Son Lansford, bass; Johnnie Lee Wills, banjo; Zeb

McNally, sax; Smokey Dacus, drums; and Tommy Duncan, vocals.

We'd no more than pulled out of Tulsa on our bus than I learned that old Jesse was the practical joker of the bunch. He was always teasing and joking, and he did it with a face full of frowns sometimes, and you really didn't know if he was serious or just being funny. That made his jokes all the more powerful.

Art was the loner. He did his job and was a fine musician. But, he minded his own business and expected you to do the same.

Leon, just eighteen, was always considered the spoiled brat. You know, like the little brother of a great big family. But he was popular and likeable. He was sort of girl crazy then and was as popular with the girls as a jug full of ice water is to a man stumbling in from the desert after five days without water.

Sleepy was one of the old troopers. He knew what Bob wanted and expected and he gave it. He also had a dry wit.

Herman was the strong man type and handled some of the heavier things like bus maintenance. He was tormented considerably by Jesse. They bickered and jawed a lot but never really got into anything serious.

Son was Bob's cousin and he always seemed to have an eye on the band. He gave me a lot of friendly advice on what to do to please Bob.

Johnnie Lee was Bob's brother. He aided me a lot at first, helping me find a place to stay. He was just an all around good fellow.

Zeb was chubby, wore glasses and was called the Judge. He looked like a portly old judge, sitting on a county court, like he always knew what the answer was and was just waiting for people to quiet down enough for him to get in with his words of wisdom.

Smokey was probably the best musician in the band at the time, if you considered his ability to read music. He knew the rudiments and expressions of music played by

26

concert groups. He sometimes caused some friction by pointing out that some of the notes were wrong or the timing was not just right. And, being an experienced drummer from "reading bands," he was critical sometimes about the boys. But he meant well and he got along with everyone.

Tommy was one of the most popular boys and probably the closest to Bob. He took a liking to me right off and I certainly knew that was to my advantage. Actually, if any of them had reason to resent me it would have been Tommy, since he was having to give up the piano in favor of me.

And, of course there was Bob, born Jim Rob Wills on March 6, 1905, in Limestone County, about fifty miles southeast of Waco, Texas. He was the firstborn of Johnnie and Emmaline Wills. He was joined by three brothers and five sisters.

The Wills family was poor and Bob was picking cotton by the time he was five. He was a helluva cotton picker. He could pick 750 pounds of cotton a day. That adds up to a bale in two days. Most people had to stretch their guts hard to get 200 pounds a day.

It was during these days in the cotton fields that Bob picked up some of his old fiddle tunes. He would listen to the Negroes picking along beside him, humming their old tunes. He never forgot them.

When Bob was eight, his father decided to move. Times were tough. The land was tough. He wanted to find something that might be easier to carve a living from. They moved west. Five hundred miles later they stopped on a small dusty farm near Turkey in Hall County, which is in Northwest Texas. Here Bob spent the rest of his childhood.

He quit school after seven years. The parching sandstorms and lean yields made hands in the fields just too valuable for school.

He picked up his first fiddle when he was nine. He did it just to show an uncle that he could play it. He had never touched one before that. But he played the hell out of it. It came natural to him.

However, he didn't really start playing the fiddle then. It was two years later when his daddy, who was supposed to play for an all-night dance at one of the ranches, failed to show up. That night Jim Rob Wills became a fiddler.

The rancher was mad at his father's absence. Bob timidly told the rancher he could play a few numbers. The rancher told him to go ahead because there were people in the crowd getting blisters from their feet itching so much to dance.

The little Wills boy picked up the fiddle and played it like it had been made for him. The crowd loved it. And, him. He went home that morning, tired but with some money in his pocket. He knew from then on that the fiddle was his musical instrument.

He played for country dances until he was sixteen. Then one night, after a huge cotton crop failure and food was lean on the table at the Wills house, Bob just slipped away without a word.

It was his first time away from home. He had no money. The only thing he knew was farming. He criss-crossed the state, doing farm work and finally he landed in Munday, Texas. A big man was standing in a group of farmers and asked if they knew where he could find a good farm hand.

"I'm the man you're looking for," said Bob, stepping forward. He was hired.

The man was Roscoe Potterage and he soon was saying that Bob, though not big, was the hardest working little man he had ever seen. Out of that relationship grew a lifetime friendship.

The Potterages had no children. Bob soon became close to them. They just sort of adopted him as their own.

They were religious people. Their faith ran as deep as the red clay that the horse drawn breaking plows split open to the sunlight. Bob soon became interested in church life.

He decided that he had led a careless, godless life and that he should change. He did. He gave his life to God.

He began preaching. One day, Mrs. Potterage had a serious talk with Bob.

"Son," she said, "we think you can do something great. And we want to help you do it. We want to send you to school . . . a seminary . . . and some day you can become a powerful minister. You can even, maybe, some day have your own church."

But he turned down the offer. He just couldn't take something from someone without working for it. He just couldn't be obligated to anyone. So he moved on.

What the ministry lost, the music world gained. Bob went home to his family and began fiddling eventually again. One night at a dance, he made up his mind. He could not be a preacher and also a musician, playing for dances and doing what he considered sinful things. But music was just too much a part of him. He had to play.

He worked a variety of jobs, barbering, working at a smelter, even shining shoes. But he kept on fiddling and he kept on getting better and better.

He got married. He tried selling insurance, selling cars, working as a surveyor, doing carpenter's work, serving as rooming house keeper. He bought a farm. He sold it and spent the money for violin lessons (they didn't last long) and barber lessons.

He barbered in New Mexico. He barbered in Turkey. But, always, it seemed the time on his other jobs cut into his music time. So he finally got a group together and began playing full time.

In 1929 he went to work for a medicine show, playing the fiddle as a blackface. He went to Fort Worth where he played over his first radio station, WBAP. Then he moved to KTAT and played there. He kept at it, picking up members in his band.

Finally, they landed a job on the program known world wide. It was "The Light Crust Doughboys." His boss was W. Lee O'Daniel, who later became governor of Texas and a U.S. senator. O'Daniel was manager of the Burrus Mill and Elevator Co., which manufactured the Light Crust Flour.

He left that company and many of his boys went with him. They went to Waco where Bob talked the manager of WACO into giving his band a spot on the station at 12:30 P.M. That manager was Everett Stover. He later became a member of Bob's band.

They moved to Oklahoma City where they began playing with Radio Station WKY. It was here that Bob and his band became known as "Bob Wills and His Texas Playboys." But, the bottom fell out. The station put on "The Light Crust Doughboys." There wasn't room for Bob.

So he took his band to Tulsa. He got some radio time on KVOO. Times were lean and rough but the band got a job at Oilton, a small town about fifty miles from Tulsa. They were to play a dance. The crowd was stupendous. Bob Wills and His Texas Playboys were on their way. They never looked back. Things kept growing and he kept getting more and more popular and everyone knew Bob Wills when they didn't even know who the governor was.

That's who was leading us in his car that day as I made my first trip with Bob Wills to Glen Oak. It was the beginning of seven years of experiences that many men with money would have given a powerful part of their personal coffers to share.

The bus we were making this trip in had been built by a man in Fort Smith, Arkansas. It had a Chevrolet motor built into its body. It made a lot of rattles and squeals and grunts. It reminded me of an old sow hog that is just about one litter away from the slaughterhouse as she tries to drag herself from her waller. She'll grunt and squeal and her old hind legs will slip some and you think sure she's not going to make it. But she does. That's the way it was with the bus. You thought for sure at times it wasn't going to make it. But it did.

The other members were really giving me a workout.

You know, trying to see if I would fit in with them. They were telling some wild stories.

"Hey, Al, we're going through a town up the road a piece and you won't believe this old gal up there," said Leon. "She beats any damn thing that I've ever heard of happening."

"What has happened to her?" I asked.

"Well, I don't know if I should tell you or not. Should I Smokey?" he replied.

Smokey just grinned.

"Tell me," I said.

Leon kept on going. Building this woman up and everything. He was getting to a real big climax. He was telling how tough and rough she was.

"Eats fistfuls of railroad spikes for breakfast," he said.

"Oh," I said.

"Yeah, she has to get the strength to take care of her youngun," he said.

"Her youngun," I said.

"Yeah, nobody ever thought that she would have a kid or give birth but sure enough she did. And guess what it was?" he asked.

"What?" I asked.

"A male gorilla," he said.

Everybody laughed loudly.

"You know who the father was?" someone roared.

"Who?" I asked.

"A male gorilla," he hollered.

I later met the girl. I must say that I wouldn't have been surprised if what they told had been true. She definitely looked like she had some gorilla blood in her.

The guys told me that the women in Oklahoma were wild over the band. So wild that they would gang up on you and take you out and rape you.

They weren't that bad. But I will say that there did seem to be plenty of them who were most agreeable to being most friendly if a man was interested.

31

"Something else you have to watch for, Al. Them men in these dance halls like the one we are going to do some powerful drinking. They get crazy drunk, and their eyes get red and watery like an old dog that's been chasing his tail in the sun all day long. And they get to wanting to beat up on us musicians because their women will smile at us and them crazy drunks don't take to that very nice at all," said one of the men.

"So what do I do?" I asked.

"Just keep your ole ass in the bus if you are afraid to fight. Just sit in here and listen to us," said one of them.

That brought another wild round of laughter.

Our old bus finally clanged into Glen Oak. And when I said Glen Oak was out in the country, I mean it was out in the country. There was maybe two families living there. One of them owned the dance hall. The sun was just dipping down into a hall of black when we arrived. There wasn't a car in sight. I thought: "How in the world is this guy Bob Wills going to pay guys like me $30 a week without any customers?"

Then I began worrying that maybe I wasn't going to get paid just like it used to always happen. I remembered a time when a bunch of us in Waco rented a hall about ten miles out in the sticks. We paid $10 for it. We started playing about 9 P.M. There wasn't anybody there. By ten, still nobody had showed up. Then we saw the lights of a car turn in and the sax man said, "Let's hit 'Dinah,' men. A car just drove up."

That's how I was feeling. Until about 8 P.M. That's when they began coming to the dance at Glen Oak. Cars were piling up outside. Some people were coming on foot. Some were riding horses. By nine, they were having to turn them away.

We started playing. Bob hadn't arrived yet. And nobody paid us much mind. About thirty minutes later, while we were playing, I heard the damndest racket I had ever heard.

There was applause, yelling and whistling. People were just going wild. Bob Wills had finally arrived.

He got up there with us and drug his fiddle out of its case. The crowd had gotten as close as they could to the bandstand. They were packed like three dozen of eggs put into a one-dozen egg container. When Bob started, the applause drowned out the music.

Bob was grinning and playing, and every so often he would point that fiddle bow of his at one of the boys and tell him to get with it. We would. And, again would come that wave of applause. Maddening. Deafening. I had never heard or seen anything like it. It wasn't a dance. It was a show. What people call today "a happening."

The boys had impressed on me during the trip up there that one of the most important things was to watch Bob at all times. You never knew when he would call on you to take it. And if he called on you and you weren't looking at him, that was the unpardonable sin.

They had also told me to smile like crazy when Bob gave me the cue and then to smile again when I had finished my break. And, there wasn't any taking a break. By that, I mean you didn't shut down the music any time. That began to hurt me. We had drunk a bunch of coffee right before the dance had started and about 11 P.M. I was crossing my legs so many times that if somebody out in the audience was watching me, they probably would have thought that I was doing the Charleston.

Finally, I leaned over to Sleepy and asked, "Sleepy, when in the hell are we going to have an intermission?"

"We don't take intermissions. If you've got to go to the bathroom, just forget it," he said.

He was right in a way. We didn't take intermissions. But, every once in awhile, one of us could get down and go back and get some relief. When that time finally came for me, I know I overstayed my allotted time in front of the trough. But man, it sure did feel good. As I was leaving, the first man in the long line behind waiting for their

33

BOB WILLS AND His Texas Playboys in September 1935. Standing left: Bob Wills; right: O. W. Mayo. Top row, left to right: Art Haines (trombone and fiddle); Son Lansford (fiddle and bass fiddle); Herman Arnspiger (guitar); Leon McAuliffe (steel guitar); Everett Stover (trumpet and announcer); Tommy Duncan (vocalist). Bottom row: Johnnie Lee Wills (banjo); Al Stricklin (piano); Smokey Dacus (drums); Pee Wee (bass); Zeb "Old Judge" McNally (saxophone); Sleepy Johnson (guitar, fiddle, banjo and bass).

THE PLAYBOYS in Cain's Academy, a popular site for dances in Tulsa, 1936.

turn, stopped me and said, "Fellow, I want to shake your hand. You skin them keys on that piano like you were peeling a stalkful of bananas." He laughed and then added, "What I am trying to say is that you are a piano player. One of the best I've ever heard!"

I don't know how I got through that night. But, I did. After it was all over, the people crowded around and kept yelling for more, and when they realized there wasn't going to be any more, they started asking for autographs. It was a long ways for a country boy from Grandview to come. I thought later as we were sopping up some chicken fried steak and cream gravy in a cafe before we headed back for Tulsa, "Man, I came awfully damn close to not coming up here. If every night is like this one, then I think I'll go kick myself in the ass for ever even thinking slightly that way."

I went to sleep happy that night. That old moon was outside our bedroom window, still pretty high in the sky considering how late it was. It looked like it was winking happiness at me.

Chapter 5

THE DAYS FLEW fast as I worked with Bob. But they were nice to me. I was getting paid every week and my wife and daughter were getting to eat pretty good, which was a lot more than many people were doing in those times.

But, even though we had our fun, we did work. And if you didn't believe in working, then there was no place for you in Bob's band. He demanded a lot of you. That was not only from your music but also from the way you conducted yourself on the bandstand. He had things for you to do in addition to your playing.

Bob not only encouraged us to be friendly to the crowd. He demanded it. He always insisted that, when we got off of the stage and went to the bathroom or outside or anywhere, we talk with the customers.

"Shake hands with them. Talk to them about their kids, aunts, crops and cattle. Because, boys, these are the people who are responsible for us being up here drawing this good money in the first place. If it wasn't for them, we all could be somewhere else, maybe eating flour gravy and biscuits three times a day and having coffee on Saturday from last Sunday's grounds," Bob said.

He believed that strongly. He believed that the crowd deserved more than just a bunch of guys getting on the stage and playing music four, five or six hours and then hightailing it on home without so much as a snicker at the audience.

So, before a dance, we would personally greet everybody we could and as fast as we could. We would learn their names and their wives' names and their children's names, so the next time we saw them, we could call them by their first name and ask how their kids were.

We did the same thing when we got down for our individual rest periods. Bob believed in us shaking as many hands as we could. We did. Many times you'd think the crowds in the restrooms were family reunions if you judged them from all the handshaking going on in there.

At first this was just a job for us. But gradually it became a pleasure. Most of us began to look forward to meeting people. And you know, now, after all these years, I can still remember many names of people I met like that.

There were some boys in the band who didn't ever really get into this type of thing. Consequently, they were never popular with the people or the band members.

A lot of these guys Bob would hire and try to work them in with the rest of us. But they just didn't work out. They were misfits.

These guys went to work with Bob just to make some money. They'd let their buddies come to hear us and play and they'd make fun of Bob and the rest of us. That was the reason they didn't like to meet the people who came to our dances. They felt like nobody but idiots would come to hear us play. They didn't believe in the music.

Bob gave these fellows a bigger chance than I ever would have. I'm not a violent man. But, if it had been me, I would have kicked them in the ass and told them to take their damn instruments and go be pied pipers for the world.

Bob didn't do it that way. He'd give them every chance

in the world. And, finally, when he saw that it wasn't going to work out, he'd call them aside. He'd talk to them. Believe me, when it reached that point, Bob knew how to talk to them boys. I overheard several of those conversations. One concerned a guy who was particularly hateful. I was standing by Bob's office door when he called the guy in.

"Well, Mr. Great Musician, I hear you don't like our music, our boys or me or our friends who come to our dances," said Bob, his dark eyes just beginning the lively dance they always went into when he was getting mad. His eyes reminded me of Indians dancing beneath a big old moon, starting off slowly to try to make it rain, but keeping at it and at it until their eyes were like coals of fire being kicked from a roaring campfire.

The man didn't say much. He just kinda grinned at first. Bob continued, "You were out of work when I put you on, Mr. Smart Britches. And, since I pay you about double what you call union scale, I guess there's only one thing to do."

The guy was beginning a nervous soft-shoe shuffle. Bob went on, "I'm giving you two weeks' pay and then you know what you can do?"

"Un-uh," said the guy.

"Get your skinny ass out of here. I don't want to see you no more. You hear me. I don't have no craving for that smart smirking face of yours. You know why?"

Actually, when Bob reached this point in his dressing down of the man, he might ask a question, but you knew from the tone of his voice, that it really wasn't a question but a statement of fact. Bob finished up: "You don't know what it's like to be a man or even a decent human being and there's another thing. In case you want to get tough like I heard you tell some of the boys, I got some information for you. I used to whip two or three asses like yours at one time. Just for exercise. Before breakfast. You understand?"

I'm sure the guy did. He left in a huff, dragging his horn behind him. And, you know what? He never lifted a finger against Bob.

In that particular case, we never saw the guy again. But we saw one of his buddies. He was a cute one. We were playing a dance at the Coliseum. There was a tremendous crowd as usual. About 10 P.M. we heard this cute idiot back in the back, hollering. He was making fun of Bob and Leon. The rest of us were getting some of his remarks too.

"I'm a good friend of that horn man you fired last week," he hollered, his voice heavy with whiskey. "You know what . . . since he's gone, you've got nothing but a bunch of corn shellers up there in the band."

He started laughing after that. All of the time he was moving closer to the bandstand, weaving in and out like a chicken snake stalking a nestful of eggs. He got to within ten feet of Leon and started making all kinds of insults.

"Yeah, Leon, baby, you take it away just like old Corn told you to. You take that corn away," he was hollering. He was laughing. "Oh, girls, isn't that Leon cute? Why, he's the greatest ladies' man in the business."

He paused, then shouted, "And, the sorriest musician. Ha, ha, ha! This whole band stinks, but Leon stinks the worst."

He was going on like this for about thirty minutes, and finally Leon looked at Bob and you could tell his eyes were begging, "Bob, can I get him?"

Bob let down his bow a minute and then said, "Leon, why don't you shut that loudmouth up?"

Leon never turned off his steel. Matter of fact, it kinda squealed when he bailed off of the stage. He was all arms and elbows. Leon was getting him.

He was pumping him in the face with his left hand (Leon is left-handed), and this guy's face was becoming like a smashed banana. In about thirty seconds, Leon turned him loose, and this guy dropped to the floor like an empty flour sack.

Leon got back on the stage and cut the squealing out of his steel and we began playing again. Everybody was laughing and they started dancing. They damn near stomped the fellow to death before he had time to get up and drag himself out. He wasn't saying nothing when he left.

As far as I can remember, we only had trouble like that one other time. I mean as a result of some musician who thought our music wasn't okay and Bob fired him.

This time when it happened we were playing a big dance again. We got the word that a guy that Bob had fired had rounded up some of his friends and they were going to give us a good whipping. The word was they would be waiting for us out on the parking lot after the dance.

We started to call the police. But then we figured that none of us had done anything to get whipped about. Besides, we decided that we could take care of ourselves. We made that request to Bob.

"Okay, boys, but, I'm going to be with you. And let's don't start anything unless they do first. Then we'll give them what they asked for," he said.

We finished our job and started out to the parking lot. Before we got there, sure enough, we saw five or six guys bunched up and as we walked by them, several of us just spoke and kept on moving. One of them said, "Look at that Sleepy Johnson. I'll bet he has to have someone hold his hand when he goes to the restroom."

"Something bothering you, mister?" asked Sleepy.

"Yeah, there is, now that you ask. I'll bet you are a brave sonofabitch when you have all of your buddies with you. Aren't you?"

"Tell you something, friend. These guys are all good buddies of mine but none of them will interfere with any fun you and I might get on with," said Sleepy.

With that, the guy started after Sleepy. Sleepy hit him

first. He really uncorked a haymaker and this guy gave a grunt and just keeled over. Two of his buddies started over. Bob said, "You fellows just hold it. This is their business so you let them finish it. Understand?"

I guess they did because they backed off. The guy that Sleepy had hit then said, "I'm finished. I've had enough. I don't want no more of this. Let's get out of here."

And, by God that's what they did. The night was filled with echoes of their feet beating a hasty retreat.

If you judge crowds' numbers by how good a band was, then there wasn't any doubt that we were good. Because we did draw some huge crowds. And people used to come up to us all of the time and say, "You boys are so good I'll bet you don't ever have to rehearse."

Nothing could have been further from the truth. You can bet your sweet bippy we rehearsed. And we rehearsed. And, we rehearsed some more.

This especially got true as Bob brought in more men and our band got larger. We had to work and work on special arrangements, scripts and orchestrations. I guess I can say that I enjoyed those rehearsals. Because I really got to know the boys good during them. Rehearsing is kinda like putting a bunch of people together in a mountain shack and then letting a blizzard snow them in for a month. They're either going to get to know each other really well and learn how to get along or they're going to have a big killing.

One thing that impressed me greatly, that I learned during the rehearsals, was Tommy Duncan's ability to memorize words to a song and forever retain them in his mind.

He would read the words about fifteen minutes. Then he'd lay the paper down, wiggle his lips for awhile, saying the words to himself. Then, brother, he had them from then on. What a memory that man had.

There was a man named Bob Ripley. He had a column in many daily papers. It was called "Ripley's Believe It or

40

Not." One time he ran in his column an item about a singer who said he knew the words to 2,000 songs. Tommy read this and blew a fuse.

"Hell, Al, I'll bet I know the words to twice that many songs. Why don't we start keeping records and just see how many I know?" he said.

So we did. I became his secretary. The project went on for about three months. We would be driving to a dance, and Tommy would think of another song he knew and he would holler it out and then say the words. We got to over 4,000 songs before we finally dropped the project.

Tommy wrote Mr. Ripley and offered to prove that he knew that many songs. But he never heard from the man. That was just one thing I learned during our rehearsals.

During these, each section would work out their arrangements. This came after the band had added horns and other instruments. The brass men would work out their parts, the reeds theirs, the rhythm men theirs and Bob and the other fiddlers would work out their own arrangements.

Sometimes our quartet would sing and then that would have to be worked into the arrangement. The same thing was true for a soloist. Then when each section was satisfied that they could do their own thing, we would fit the whole band together on the number. Bob did his arranging as he played at a dance or show.

That's kinda how the rehearsals went. Believe me when we walked into a dance hall, we not only were prepared to shake everyone's hands including the dog that was over pissing on the tree, but we were ready to play music.

We played music at many places. And I remember practically all of them. But I don't guess any of them hold fonder or more vivid memories than Cain's Academy. That first night there was really an education. I thought I had seen about everything. But, as was to happen so many times during my career with Bob, I hadn't seen nothing yet.

Cain's Academy got its name from its original purpose

41

of being built. That was for the instruction of dancing. It was only later that they started having ballroom dancing to pick up extra money.

It was housed in an old native stone building that had a gradual sloping roof. The front of the building was nearly on the main street of Tulsa with only a small sidewalk in front separating the building from the traffic.

There was a large parking lot space about the size of two ordinary city blocks on one side of Cain's. It never held all of the crowd that came to the dances. Consequently, their cars spilled out all along the streets.

The inside of the building had only one row of seats. These stretched in a continual line around all sides of the dance floor. Really, when we played, very few people sat down. Most would be standing and watching us or they would be out there dancing.

We played a lot of our noon broadcasts there. During those times they would start bringing out folding chairs and would keep putting them down until they had enough. Sometimes it took 500 chairs.

Inside of Cain's and down at one end was a long, L-shaped bar. There were no chairs in front of it. They had no waitresses to take drinks to tables — because they didn't have any tables. At that time, the only legal alcoholic beverage in Oklahoma was 3.2 beer. So when people wanted a beer or a soft drink, they just bellied up to that old wooden bar.

We arrived early as usual and mixed and mingled with the crowd. Everyone seemed glad to see me aboard with the band, and that made me feel good. Several offered me drinks. Of course at most of those dances, people would offer a mad elephant a drink. So I don't guess that was saying too much.

While we were getting ready to play that night, I made a discovery that I was to make many times during the next few months with the band. That discovery came at the piano. It wasn't worth a damn. I doubt very much if a

42

junkyard dealer would even have wanted it for his parlour. If he had, it would have been only to look at it. Because it sure didn't offer much in the way of playing.

The reason for this was because of Tommy Duncan. As you know, Bob hired me to play the piano. Before he did that, Tommy was his piano player. By Tommy's own admission, he made sort of a game out of tearing pianos up.

"Al," he once told me, "I don't know a helluva lot about playing a piano. But I'm a real professional when it comes to tearing them up."

He didn't mean on a break. He meant what he said. Tearing the piano up. Literally. He would beat them with his fist, take off his boot and pound them with his boot-heel. He would take a stick and rake it up and down the keys.

Before he knew it, there would be a crowd over there watching him and cheering him on. He really didn't need the cheering. But it helped him anyway.

"Come on Tommy, tear that damned thing up," they'd holler.

Tommy would oblige. Sometimes he would get so carried away that the hammers would start breaking out. Tommy would sit there grinning and dodging the keys as they came flying out at him.

I don't intend to downgrade the memory of Tommy Duncan when I tell about how he played the piano. He did what he had to do to entertain the people. He got many laughs. Besides, many of them were already old wrecks when he got to them. They deserved the punishment he gave them. He sure wasn't stingy with it.

I had just made my assessment of the piano that night, and I was pleasantly surprised. Tommy may have torn one up, but the one there was in good shape. So maybe they had repaired it.

Bob started playing with us that night from the very first. There were more people dancing that night because a lot of people there saw Bob twice a week and they wanted

43

to take advantage of the chance to dance to his music.

I had seen a good many dances, but nothing like that night. Some of the couples were in their seventies. Some were teen-agers. Some were graceful. Some were as clumsy as a man trying to walk up a sand dune with railroad ties tied to his shoes. But, they all were dancing.

Women were dancing with other women. Some were dancing by themselves. All were just moving and moving and sometimes stopping and hollering for more. They were having the time of their lives.

There were many beautiful girls out there that night. Gosh, I never knew that the country had so many pretty women. They were all looking and eying the band as they always did.

Leon, always popular with the women, was as busy as a one-legged man in an ass-kicking contest. He kept up the smiling at the girls and all of the time keeping that watchful eye on Bob to be sure he didn't miss his break.

We played a schottische number and I'll bet you there were two dozen varieties of the schottische being done out there on the floor. Those feet were going down in a resounding "thump, thump, thump-thump-thump." Those old walls were ringing with good times.

I was having a good time too. Bob really featured me all night long. He kept saying, "And now, here's our new piano player, Al Stricklin."

Away I would go and it was truly a wonderful night. I thought the world was a nice place to live in. "Lord, just keep on giving me these good pianos," I said to myself.

Two of the band's most faithful friends and patrons in Tulsa were Hugh Davis and his beautiful little wife. They were so perfect for each other, such good dancers, and had wonderful personalities. They were the kind of people that if you were caught out in a rain and got soaking wet and came in to change and you discovered the roof had sprung a leak and your change of clothes was wet too,

44

they could make it seem like you were putting on dry clothes.

Hugh was the curator and manager of the zoo at Tulsa. Both he and his wife were experts on animals. Many times, Mrs. Davis came to our broadcast with a pet monkey or some other kind of pet that she wanted to show off.

Admiral Byrd made a three-month trip to the North Pole in the 1930s. Hugh was selected as one of the experts to go along with them. He was selected as the specialist to study animal life. The Davises kept in touch during his absence by shortwave radio.

Hugh, who weighed about 165 pounds, was in perfect physical condition. He could hold his own in a fight, but fighting was the furthest thing from his mind because he liked people so much.

However, one night at Cain's, the Davises were dancing, gracefully as usual, and as they danced near the bandstand, they waved and smiled at all of us as they always did. Just about that time, the biggest, meanest, and ugliest looking sonofabitch I've ever seen came along and said to Hugh's wife, "Baby, I want to dance with you."

"Thank you, but no," she said, smiling all of the time.

The bad guy just grunted and grabbed her out of Hugh's arms. He started dragging her across the floor. She was screaming, "Hugh! Hugh! Sweetheart . . . help me!"

It didn't take Hugh long to react. He started running and caught up with them. He kinda parted them and then planted a good uppercut on this guy's chin. Just as he was hitting the floor, his buddy came running over. He was even bigger and uglier. He was shouting obscenities. He let loose with a haymaker. Hugh ducked. Then he floored him.

The other one had stumbled to his feet in the meantime, and he was hollering crazy things. Hugh decked him. Then the second guy was up again. Hugh decked him.

The crazy part of the whole thing was that Hugh never got hit a time. He was doing a fine job. Such a fine job that

Bob and all of us were just caught up in admiring what was going on and as a result, Bob forgot to tell the bouncer to step in and stop it.

In between the solid licks he was throwing, Hugh would look up to Bob and say, "I'm sorry for this disturbance."

There would follow a "lickety whop" and then Hugh would say again, "I'm sorry for this, Bob."

"Lickety whop."

Until finally, those two bullies had enough and they started helping each other out of the building. I'll never forget the second one saying as he drug his buddy out, "The next damn time you want to dance, you pick someone who ain't got no date, or I'm going to whip hell out of you."

There were a lot of good people who worked at Cain's. One was Howard Turner, the dance instructor. He more or less went with the place when Bob bought it. He did that when Mr. Cain, called "Daddy" by everyone who knew him, became ill and said he wanted to sell it to Bob.

After Bob purchased Cain's, he kept Howard on to teach dancing and perform other duties. Howard was kinda nervous and fidgety, but he was very friendly and likeable.

I nearly had a disaster one night at Cain's. That happened because of Smokey's habit of flipping cigarette butts onto the piano keyboard. He started doing that soon after I started playing with the band and he never stopped it.

Our sitting positons on the bandstand at Cain's gave him a real good shot at the piano. It was at such an angle that I had to look away from the piano much of the time in order to keep watching Bob in case he wanted me to take a break on the piano. Many times as I was watching Bob and playing, I would feel this sudden burn on my fingers. I would look down and there would be one of Smokey's cigarettes. I never got to where it didn't scare the hell out of me.

But that night at Cain's, Smokey was flipping those

46

cigarettes by the dozens. That was one night you can say I was burning the keyboard up. Apparently, one of them fell down through the keyboard.

We actually didn't realize it had happened until we came back to work Monday. There was no piano left. It was just a pile of metal parts. It had burned up.

We played many regular spots, like Cain's. Another place was Fort Smith, Arkansas. That first trip I made to Fort Smith was a corker. It was a long one too. It was 140 miles and on that old bus and with those bad roads, that were mostly dirt that sifted through the windows, I can't say it was all pleasure.

When we arrived in Fort Smith, people were stopping and looking and waving. They were smiling and letting loose with Bob's "ahh-haas." The whole damned town seemed to know we were there.

One of my duties was to help Tommy carry the public address system in and get it set up. This had to be done as soon as possible in order to get ahead of the crowd.

The place we played at Fort Smith was called the Winter Garden. To get into it, you had to climb a set of wooden stairs.

Those were the longest and most straight-up stairs I had ever seen. The speakers for the PA must have weighed eighty pounds. We also had the amplifiers, cords and other paraphernalia. It was about seven-thirty by this time. The dance started at nine.

We just thought we were getting ahead of the crowd. There were already about 600 people packed into the hall. It held 1200. I started trying to imagine what it was going to be like by the time the dance started.

As we were trying to hang up the speakers, I could hear people saying, "I bet that is Al Stricklin, that new piano player."

I felt like a dignitary. I felt like I was in a dream and would wake up. Just a few days ago, I was a nobody. No one had ever heard of me. Now here these people were looking and talking and repeating my name.

I again realized the magic of Bob Wills. Who else could have worked up that kind of reputation so quick for a guy like me.

Later, just before the dance was to start, I was sounding notes for the various boys to tune their instruments by. That's when I made a discovery. The Winter Garden had no windows. In those days, there was no such thing as air conditioning. I looked up. There wasn't even an old overhead whirling fan. There was nothing to move any air.

The only door was down on the ground floor at the foot of the stairs. I have always been hot natured. I sweat when its colder than a well digger's ass in Montana. So I knew we were in for trouble. Rather, I was in for trouble.

Before we even hit a note, I was wet with sweat. Bob was a sweater too. He often would take along a change of clothes so he could change before heading back home. I later did the same thing. But, I didn't have any spare clothes that night.

The people were jammed inside. They helped the temperature climb. Then it hit me — all of a sudden like. "This is a funny goddamn name for this place . . . Winter Garden."

There were 360 unescorted women that night at the dance. I think every one of them was banked around the bandstand. Every time you looked at one of them, she would give you that sweet Arkansas smile, like she was saying, "Here I am baby. Come and get me." Apparently, they didn't get turned off by a sweater. And, me being human, I soon forgot about the heat. I had never had so many good-looking women giving me such approving glances.

Things like that worked to Bob's advantage. It helped him get the most out of the band. I look back on it now and it reminds me of the way we used to burn rubber on those old Fords back in the good old days. You just wanted

48

to show off with all of the women looking at you.

Some months later, when we were back at Fort Smith, something happened concerning women that I'll never forget. On that occasion we were spending the night. There was a big celebration in town going on and we were the featured attraction.

The hotel we were in was full of people. There were all kinds. Farmers in starched-up overalls. Businessmen in suits. Women in flowing dresses. Country girls in dresses made from feed sacks.

We were trying to get some rest and some girls came up to the floor we were on. They went to one of the boys' doors and knocked.

"Is this Bob Wills' room?" one asked in a giggling voice.

"Young lady, you are in luck. I am Bob Wills. And, believe me, you have really hit the jackpot. Do you know who that is over there?" he asked, pointing to his roommate.

"No, sir, I surely don't," said one of the girls.

"Well, that is Leon McAuliffe," said the band member.

The two girls just burst out giggling. They were so excited at finding not only Bob Wills, but Leon too. They could hardly contain themselves.

"May we, uh, may we have your autographs?" one of them asked.

"Why certainly," one of the band members replied.

"You just come on in here and we'll give you our autographs and anything else you might be interested in."

I don't know what happened next. But I do know one thing. The boys never learned those girls' names. And the girls never learned the boys' real names. I'll tell you one thing, though. They sure as hell were not Bob Wills and Leon McAuliffe.

That's what made things so great about playing with Bob. You just never knew what was going to happen next. It was what made me happy. It was also what made me realize how lucky I was when I was reading the newspapers

49

and saw such things as an advertisement run by a young couple who obviously were out of work. They sounded desperate. They said:

We want any kind of work . . . anywhere.

Or I read things about a firm hunting a salesman to sell groceries. The work was six days a week. The pay was $100 a month.

But things were looking up a little. One story told about the stock market being stimulated by further hopes of a broadening peace in Europe. The market had climbed a little.

I was like the market. I was climbing. But, I didn't have to climb too far. Because I felt like I was already in the top of a big tree. I had me a real stout limb to sit on.

Chapter 6

I T WAS THE 1930s. The people were hungry. Many were out of work. There were little movie houses studded around the squares of the small towns. You got in for a nickle. Sometimes less. You brought your own popcorn and probably, if you lived in the country, you grew that yourself.

There were no television sets. People didn't even know what television was. But, there was radio. It was entertainment, though often all you got while listening to one of the little tiny boxes was a harsh scratching static that resembled newscasts and sometimes music and sometimes a suspense show.

But, radio helped us tremendously. We were broadcasting every day at noon. The people would come in from their farming and ranching, and while sopping up corn bread and butter and cane syrup and beans and fried potatoes, they would listen to Bob Wills and His Texas Playboys. When we were in their town, they scraped up all of the money they could to come and see us. Sometimes I would look at them people out there in the audience and I would figure that their fingernails must have been blunted from having to scrape the bottom of the barrel so much just to exist.

You turn a bunch of people loose in a great vast dance hall and start playing music that they like, and you are going to see some luxurious kicking up of the heels. People dancing are bound to start drinking. And hollering, and just having a big time and sometimes they might get a bit unruly. With the size of our crowds that could have been a problem. But Bob, thinking of everything, planned for that. He hired John Briggs.

Briggs was a former wrestling champion. He kinda hit upon bad times after that and he was pretty hard up when Bob hired him. He appreciated it very much. I believe that he would have walked thorugh fire for Bob.

I think he had the finest set of muscles that I've ever seen. His arms rippled like big snakes coiling up when he just barely flexed them. He was a stud.

Normally, he would stand by the bandstand with his eyes on Bob. If a disturbance broke out and it looked like it was going to get out of hand, Bob would give Briggs the nod. Presto. That was the end of one disturbance. He never backed down or away. I don't think he knew what being afraid was supposed to mean.

I remember one time we were playing at the Blue Moon, an outdoors place in Tulsa. There were about eight men there in a tight little group and they were living it up pretty high. They kept drinking, and finally they got to jawing at each other and before you knew it, one of them hit one of the others. That's all it took. Suddenly, they were all really getting with it.

Then some more started joining in and it looked like it was going to get out of hand. You know, a gang fight. One of those can ruin a public gathering. It can have bad effects on the band too, I mean if someone swings at his antagonizer and the antagonizer is standing close to the bandstand and he ducks and — well, like I said, it can have a bad effect on the band.

52

Anyway, Bob let this go on as long as he could and then he gave old Briggs the nod. Briggs didn't wait. He bowed his head and waded into that gang of toughs, just like a lumberjack picking up an axe and heading for a towering redwood.

I was a bit afraid for Briggs at first. From my vantage point, I could see everything. Those guys he was marching into were no little fellows. It didn't matter to Briggs.

He sorta zigzagged through those guys, punching here, stepping back there, punching again, and all of the time moving forward. In what seemed less than a minute he was on the other side and he was the only one left standing. The rest were sprawled out on the floor. I remember hearing an old rancher say, "By Gawd, Mama, he hit them fellows as quick as that old mule kicks me when I'm plowing."

Briggs was a physical fitness freak. He was always jumping up and down and doing push-ups or sit-ups. When he was riding, he would be pulling on something to give his muscles a workout. No wonder that he was so well built.

Anyway, Bob decided that the band wasn't doing too good, physically. He thought we were getting out of shape and that might lead to us getting colds or something which would lead to us having to miss playing. All that led to Bob thinking that doing setting-up exercises every day would be a good idea. He put Briggs in charge.

After rehearsal each day, Briggs would come in. He had a funny characteristic. Here he was, this man-mountain who could probably whip King Kong, and yet he had a high-pitched, little squeaky voice. It sounded like a woman's. Anyway, he would line us up, and then shout, "Okay, men, let's get started!"

We would start our exercising. We would do push-ups. We would do sit-ups. We would do side straddle hops. All of the time this would be going on a lot of the boys would be breaking wind, and Briggs would holler, "Okay, you boys cut that out!"

53

Bob exercised with us. To keep the hours he kept, and live the life he led, he was in real good physical condition. So he seemed to enjoy the exercising.

The exercising lasted for about three weeks. Then the guys began to find excuses to miss the exercising. Some would say they had a cold. Some would say they had an upset stomach. Some wouldn't say anything. At least not to Briggs' face. They just wouldn't show up.

Briggs kept at them. He said, "You boys exercise like I tell you and someday you'll have muscles just like me."

"Hell!" I mumbled. "We wouldn't have muscles like you if we worked at it half a lifetime."

So it stopped. But Bob kept after it. He kept up his exercise program for a long time with Briggs always assisting him. Briggs was a nice guy. He came in handy in ways other than handling the crowd. One time that happened in Joplin, Missouri. Our dances there were usually sponsored by the fire department. One of the firemen was named Ed. He was as friendly and gracious a person as you'd ever want to meet. But he had a habit we didn't like.

Everytime he saw us, he had to shake hands with us. Didn't matter if you'd been gone for only a day, when Ed saw you he wanted to shake hands. That was the problem. When Ed shook hands with you, he really shook hands. He'd grab your fingers and dang near break them. Many times my hands felt like they'd been run over by a tractor after old Ed let go of them. All the time he was doing this, he would be smiling. We often talked about having to go to the chiropractor to have our knuckles adjusted so we could play again.

I could never figure out why he did that unless he was trying to impress us with his strength. It got so bad that we started dodging old Ed. We figured that we didn't have time to go see a doctor before every dance.

One day someone got the idea to tell Briggs about our problem. We did. He started shaking his head up and down and said, "Well, I will see what I can do."

54

That night Briggs walked up to Ed, stuck out his hand and said, "Hello, Ed. Long time no see."

Ed smiled. He tried to get Briggs by the fingers. But Briggs was quick. He got Ed's fingers first. The match was on.

I swear you could hear crunching and grinding, like someone had locked two old cars together with log chains to see which one could outpull the other. Finally, Ed started getting tears in his eyes. He relaxed his grip. He didn't say a word. He walked away. He had good reason. His hand hurt. And he had to go change his britches. Briggs had squeezed the shit out of him. Literally. We never had any more trouble with Ed shaking hands like he had a steel vice in his hand. He did it right. After the match with Briggs. And, before long, we forgave him for his earlier squeezing.

Briggs wasn't the only good man Bob had in his organization. He had a lot of good people. Another one was O. W. Mayo, Bob's business manager. He was not only a good person, but he was a character.

Seemed like he was always chewing tobacco, rolling it around in his jaw and letting fly with brown streams of juice. He loved to fish and hunt and play golf and on our days off, Mayo tried to spend them with us.

Mayo had a way of selling Bob's band to total strangers. He also could make deals with big companies and institutions which resulted in money in the band's pocket.

He had a big influence in making the deal with the Red Star Milling Company of Wichita, Kansas. They milled our flour. When I say that, I mean the "Playboy Flour." It was their best flour. A bakery later put their best bread in our wrappers and it was sold as "Playboy Bread."

Mayo sometimes would talk to a wayward member of the band who he felt was out of line. He wasn't the boss. Bob was the boss and there was no doubt about that. But Mayo took up some slack many times. I've heard him lay the law down to lots of guys.

He made many trips with us. He took the teasing and rough stuff just like any other member, always chewing that tobacco and looking at you with those eyes that had wisdom like an owl.

Sometimes when a band member had a problem and he didn't think it was big enough to bother Bob with, he would go to Mayo. And always out came that wisdom. I can speak personally of this, because he gave me some of the best advice that I've ever received.

It was on a touchy matter that came about as the result of a wreck my wife and one-year-old daughter had. The car was damaged heavily. They weren't hurt seriously, but their injuries were painful.

The man who hit them was in an oil company car and had liability insurance. He admitted quickly to a witness that he was at fault. The insurance agent came to me and told me to get bids on the car repair, taxi fares and anything that we were out. He said his company would pay everything.

Well, I told that to the doctor. He said, "You want to make a small fortune out of this?"

"What do you mean?" I asked.

"You know these kind of injuries can malinger. You know, drag on. They can cost a lot of money," said the doctor. He winked at me.

It was tempting. I was making $45 a week and living in a duplex that had noisy kids next door who kept me from sleeping a lot of times. I needed some new clothes. Maybe a boat. A better car and money for my daughter's education.

It really got to worrying me. Then one day I went to Mayo and laid it out on the line for him. I told him just how it was and asked him what he'd do.

It was a Sunday afternoon and Mayo was fooling around in his yard. He was chewing that tobacco.

He asked me how my wife and baby were doing. I told him they were doing okay. He asked me about my car. I told him that it hadn't been totaled after all and it would be fixed in a few days.

He didn't say anything for a long time. He kept fooling around with some flowers and he bent down and smelled them. He said, "My those smell pretty."

He chewed his tobacco and then he continued, "Al, I like you very much. Bob and the rest of the boys like you, too. We all feel that you came to us as kinda an educated man, someone who children had respect for and would look up to. All of us feel that you are one of the boys in the band who would be honest. One we could trust, like a person that you could go to sleep with and your billfold in sight and wake up and find it still there. Of all the boys, if I had to pick one that I felt would really have a conscience, it would be you."

He shifted his tobacco to the other side of his jaw, bent down and smelled the flowers again and continued, "Now, Al, as soon as your wife and baby have finished with the doctor and all those expenses you mentioned are turned in to the insurance company and you get your compensation, and you know in your heart that nothing bad will happen from all this, are you going to be able to look the world in the eye and say, 'I'm Al Stricklin, an honest man'? Furthermore, I don't believe all the people in this organization would still feel quite the same way if you go for big money with this company."

I felt like a big load had been lifted from my shoulders. I knew what I had to do. What I should do. I turned in my itemized statement a few days later for something like $900 and signed my release in return for the insurance company's check.

The agent called me and said, "Mr. Stricklin, it has been a most enjoyable pleasure to work with you and it is nice to know there are honest people left in this country. You had my company over a barrel and many people would have sued us for thousands and probably have gotten it."

That made me feel good. Maybe that's why right after

Mayo gave that advice that day, I bent over and those flowers smelled like a field of ambrosia.

But Mayo wasn't the only good person in Bob's organization. As I said, there were many. One was his secretary. Her name was Ada. Man, what a girl! She was everybody's friend and helper. She kept books, made out payrolls, wrote letters, answered the phone and was just an all around Girl Friday.

She had to be a mind reader, a politician and a diplomat all in one. I never saw her get angry. She had this one fault. Actually, it wasn't a fault. She blushed a lot. We used to tease her just to see her blush. Her face would turn as red as a tomato ready for picking.

She never had been married. When she finally did make the big jump, she married Alvin Perry, the man who ran the concession at Cain's. He was a prince of a guy, too.

Really, getting good people was Bob's way of doing things. He knew how valuable they were to keep an organization flowing smoothly. His ambition was to build a great organization. If one of his brothers got in the way of progress, he went. If one of his boys got in the way of progress, he went. Nothing and nobody interfered with the headway of his organization as it drove to greatness. His determination to make it that way brings to focus another event. It happened because of what Bob required us to do while on the bandstand.

I've mentioned that already. He wanted us to show enthusiasm and smile at the customers. Naturally, some of these customers were good-looking women. Some were horrible looking. But they were all paying customers and Bob wanted us to give them their money's worth.

Anyway, at the first, some of the wives of the band members would come to the dances at Cain's Academy on Thursday and Saturday nights. They also made some of the other dances. They liked the music, but they wanted to keep their husbands in line.

Sure enough if a husband was caught smiling at a

58

woman, he caught holy hell when he got home. It got pretty bad, so bad that Bob noticed that some of the boys would be acting like they had lost their last friend. Bob would point that fiddle bow at a clarinet player and with his big smile would say, "Sell it man, sell."

Yet, there would be that man looking like the last rose of summer. He would not be smiling. He would not be looking at Bob. He would be worrying about his wife watching him. He didn't want to catch hell again.

Bob kept getting madder and madder about the situation. He finally reached the point to where he was boiling. But he didn't say anything until after an incident happened one night at Cain's.

This girl, who came nearly every time we played, was there. She had on an expensive fur coat. She sat close to the bandstand, directly in line with one of our musicians. She came up and spoke to me and smiled, because I was sitting just below the musician she was in line with. When she spoke, this musician waved at somebody else in the crowd.

His wife saw him smile and wave just at the time the girl was smiling and saying hello to me. She just knew they were flirting around. She didn't waste any time. She bolted from her chair and tore right into the middle of this woman talking to me. She was as innocent as a newborn babe. But the musician's wife didn't know that. She was beating the hell out of her.

"I've got you at last, you damn home-breaking bitch," she hollered, all of the time pounding the paying customer. She finally was restrained and carried bodily from the hall.

We knew that something drastic was going to happen from Bob. It did the next day after our broadcast. He let us have it. We were all standing around with our heads kinda bowed when Bob began. He said, "I started this band and I didn't have a pot to piss in. I worked hard. I lived

ANOTHER POSED PHOTO in Cain's Academy, Tulsa, 1936.

AUGUST, 1935—The Playboys fly from Tulsa, Oklahoma to Waco, Texas. This was Bob Wills' first and only flight.

close and a lot of times I didn't eat. I didn't bathe. And I wore worn-out clothes."

He kept on going, telling about how he had worked this band to the top — to where we were making good money and drawing good crowds. Then he said, "The chain is as strong as its weakest link."

By now, his face was red and a little spot on the back of his neck about the size of a silver dollar had turned as red as a monkey's butt. That's when you knew Bob was really mad. When that spot got red, you'd better watch. He was practically shouting by now. He said, "By God, fellows, as of this minute, there will not be one more wife of a musician at any dance I play for — ever! If I have to play by myself because of a bunch of sissy, pantywaist, hen-pecked, half-assed musicians, who can't control their wives, then by God, I will play by myself. The music would sound better with you not even there than the way you have been working. Starting tonight, if one of your wives is seen at a dance, the next day, you get your two weeks' pay and get out.

"I know what every one of your wives is going to think of me, but let me tell you something — I don't give a damn what they think. No damned jealous, suspicious woman, belonging to any man, is going to tear down what it has taken me fifteen years to build up. If you think I am fool-ing about this, just let your wife show up at one more dance. You will see who's fooling."

We knew he wasn't fooling. No more wives showed up at the dances for awhile. The boys got back into the groove and our music picked up considerably. The master had spoken.

When you considered how Bob handled that and how he had to handle all of the different characters in the band, you really appreciated his leadership. One of those charac-ters was an Italian named Tiny Mott. He was single and if there was anything he liked better than making music

60

with his sax and clarinet, it was girls. It was hard to tell which came first.

He would see some real sharp chick while we were playing and his black hair would begin sweating with desire. Women really gave him a fit. It turned into a near disaster for him one night when we were playing a Sadie Hawkins Dance for the University of Arkansas.

During those dances, the young people would dress up like Daisy Mae and Li'l Abner. The boys would go barefoot and wear old tattered jeans. The girls wore cut-off jeans that would make the hot pants of today look like ice cubes. Around their bosoms they only wore a narrow cloth about equal to a scarf.

At this particular dance, the girls were pushing all around the bandstand and keeping time with the music with their feet. Their bosoms were — well they were keeping a nice kind of time, too, as they bounced up and down.

The band started running high temperatures. It was especially bad for the sax men since they had mouthpieces in their mouths. It was particularly bad for Tiny Mott.

With hundreds of Daisy Maes dancing in front of him, he simply went berserk. The guys on either side of him had to keep pushing him back into his chair. And all of the time he was chewing on his reed. He kept chewing them up. He kept asking for spares. By the time that dance was over, we figured that Tiny had set a new world's record for chewing up reeds. He chewed up eight.

There were a lot of interesting things that happened to us at Fayetteville. We played there about once every six weeks. One night while we were playing, another band was playing at another place. It was what we called a "legit" band. They read music and thought our band was just a bunch of freaks.

We played to a capacity crowd that night. The "legit" band had so few paid customers that they gave up about 10:30. After we got through, we went to an all-night cafe to eat. The other band was already there. They recognized us when we walked in.

They were already disturbed because we had outdrawn them. I imagine they had been giving us the bad news before we even got there. When we walked in, one of them said, "Well, look who's here, Bob Wills and His Texas *Plowboys*. Eleven banjos, a guitar, and what a guitar."

Bob usually ignored such remarks. He didn't this time. He walked over and looked at the guy and said, "You know son, nobody likes us but the people."

That was one of the most descriptive remarks I ever heard. I have never been able to come closer to it in trying to put across what Bob Wills and his music meant to the crowds.

The young man got up and came over. He looked ashamed and told Bob that he was sorry. Then his leader came over and introduced himself.

"Mr. Wills, I have always wanted to meet you. I think you are great." He paused a minute and then added, "I'll tell you something else. If my agent ever books me in this area again and I find out that Bob Wills is within one hundred miles, I'm going to tell him to go to hell. I'm not going to accept that booking."

There was one thing about us. We would accept bookings anywhere. One place was in a remote place in Kansas called Corona. An Italian couple ran this place. The community was made up mostly of Italian-Americans. They were fine people.

This couple who ran the dance had a big bunch of children. One was a cute little fellow about seven. He loved to stand right in front of the mike where Bob, Tommy and the fiddlers worked. He would plant himself right there in front of the mike when we started and he didn't leave until we were through for the night.

He would just grin and his dark eyes would sparkle as he watched us work. He never looked away. Jesse decided to play a joke on the little boy.

62

En route to Corona, he ate a big batch of raw garlic at a little cafe. He mixed chile and hot pepper with this, and the result was the stinkingest breath I ever smelled. It kept getting worse as the miles rolled by.

By the time we started the dance, you could smell Jesse all over the building. If you got near him, you would cry. I told him, "Jesus, Jesse, your breath would change the thoughts of a horny mule to running for the river!"

Well of course when the music started that night, our little fan was there, smiling and looking at us from his perch in front of the band. After about thirty minutes, Jesse stepped down and got right in the little boy's face. He repeated this contact many times during the night.

The little kid never moved. He just smiled. Not once did he turn his head. Now, that was what I call a dedicated fan.

We had dedicated fans everywhere. There were bunches of them at Seminole, Oklahoma. That was one of our favorite places to play. The crowds were good, the people were courteous and receptive.

Like all places, Seminole had guys who always wanted us to have a drink with them. One night we were down there and me and another band member were back in the men's room. Bob had given us an order earlier that there was to be no drinking. But this fellow came into where we were, and he offered us a drink. I declined. The other band member didn't. He had a drinking problem. A bad drinking problem.

The fellow handed him a pint. The seal was not broken. The musician broke it and turned it up. He didn't stop until half of it was gone.

He started to hand it back.

"Hell, man you go ahead and get all you want," said the customer. The musician tilted the bottle again. He finished it, handing the empty bottle back to the man.

"Goddamn. You must have had a powerful thirst," said the customer. "But don't worry. I've got some more."

I hope he did.

We had another unusual experience at Seminole. We flew there one time to fill our date. We rode in an old ten-place Stinson Tri-Motor.

On that day, as we often did when we were going to fly somewhere, we told the folks over the radio that we were coming by plane to their city. We told them that if they brought a "Playboy" bread wrapper and $3 they could ride in our plane.

We called it our plane because our name was painted on the sides with musical notes. When we landed that day, hundreds of people were lined up to greet us. They had fistfuls of bread wrappers and jars full of money so they could ride in the plane. I remember seeing one man waiting to crawl onto the plane. He said just before he got aboard, "Flying today and hearing Bob Wills tonight! I can die happy now."

Bob only flew with us once. That was from Tulsa to Waco. It was a thrill he never repeated. It happened before I went to work for him. He told me about it one time when I was riding with him in his car.

"The boys talked me into it, Goddamn them," he related. "I never wanted to fly before that, and afterwards I never wanted to fly again."

He said he was nervous during the entire trip. He couldn't talk. He would look down and see little fleecy clouds floating by and he just didn't think he should be up above them looking down.

"I'd a helluva lot rather see their bellies than their backs," he said.

The boys were laughing and cutting up. They kept teasing Bob. But he couldn't see anything funny about it. Then Earl Field, our pilot, who had been a World War I fighter pilot, announced that they were close to Waco. Everyone looked out of the window and they could see hundreds of people waiting for them.

At about 500 feet altitude, Earl banked and zoomed the

plane and then wiggled the wings to signify a greeting. Bob came unglued.

"What's the matter? What the hell is happening?" he shouted.

"Old Earl's waving his wings with a greeting to the people," one of the band members explained.

"Wave and greeting, hell! Let him do the damn greeting when he gets down on the ground!" screamed Bob.

When he got down, he said he would never fly again. He never did.

Things like the big tri-motor with our name painted on it and our radio show and our smiling at people and our music caused our fame to spread. And sometimes it helped. Matter of fact, it saved Tommy Duncan's life many times. I mean him being in Bob Wills' band and the band being so well known.

During our playing, Pretty Boy Floyd, the gangster, was in his heyday. His name and face were plastered all over the front pages of newspapers. Everyone, or practically everyone, knew what he looked like. That was where the problem came in for Tommy. You see, he looked just like Pretty Boy Floyd.

I'll never forget the first time he was mistaken for Pretty Boy. He was out on his day off riding around. He had eased up to a stop sign. A police car was parked beside him. Tommy gunned away and pulled into a service station. Right behind him was the police car. Suddenly two more showed up. They were out with their guns drawn.

"Oh, damn, what have I committed?" Tommy murmured to himself.

The officers came over. They asked him to get out, then said, "Get out Pretty Boy. With your hands in the air."

"Pretty Boy?" asked Tommy. "Well, I ain't exactly pretty, but the girls always think I'm good-looking."

"Pretty Boy Floyd," said the officer. "Get out. We know who you are."

That's when Tommy cut out the nonsense and told them

65

who he really was. He said, "I'm a Texas Playboy. I play for Bob Wills."

He showed them his musician's card. They finally believed him. He came back the next day and laughed about it. But it happened several times.

We always thought it was funny. We always laughed about it. But times were being good to us. We were the Texas Playboys. We were having fun. And not only were we thrilling the crowds, we were making recordings too. Those resulted in some wild times.

Chapter 7

WE LOVED OUR recording sessions. We got extra money for playing, which was something always good to have in the thirties. Getting an extra dollar then was like getting a second blob of butter on your biscuits. It was appreciated.

But we also loved the frolic of big proportions that went on when we recorded.

The first recording session I made with Bob was on September 23 and 24 in 1935, in Dallas. Actually, it was the first recording session for Bob with his own outfit. He had made a few records as a Light Crust Doughboy before, but he had never made a recording as Bob Wills and His Texas Playboys.

We really worked our tails off getting ready for the session. Bob ran in a lot of rehearsals just for the occasion. So by the time the date got there, we were primed and ready.

There were two men running the recording studio. They were Englishmen. Natives is what I mean. At least their accents made them seem like natives of England. They were Art Satherly and Don Law. Right after we met them, Satherly said, "I say, old boys, it's a cheery good morning and we've got lots on the schedule. So hip, hip."

67

He spit that sentence out like it was one of today's 45 rpm records being played 78 and his voice had that pinch to it, cutting his words like they were from a well manicured lawn. One of the band members said, "Say, would you go over that one more time and just a little more slowly so I can catch that beat. I've never heard one like that before. Is it four-four or something else?"

We all laughed. The Englishmen kinda frowned at first. Matter of fact, they frowned a lot for awhile because they simply had never heard or seen anything like our band.

They had made the contract because of our growing popularity. They were wealthy, highly educated and sophisticated. In other words, I don't imagine they ever wore white socks with black britches. So no doubt they expected to hear something like Tommy Dorsey's band.

They just looked and then in a very cool and calculated way they told us to get tuned up.

"I say, old boys, play something so we can get us a balance, you know," said one of them.

We tuned our instruments, and suddenly Bob began tapping his boot and kicked off with "The Osage Stomp." That's a loud, exuberant old tune and we really let it all out. It had amazed me when I first heard it. It amazed the Englishmen. Mr. Satherly began screaming, "Hold it! Hold it! Hold it, gentleman. We can't get a balance on that. You are not hitting the thump, thump together."

We got quiet and he said, "Is this what the American people want to hear?"

Mr. Mayo, chewing his tobacco as usual, had a coffee cup in his hands and he spit into it, then said, "You bet, pardner. That's what is drawing them crowds that you've been hearing so much about."

We had a little talk then, and before long we had the Englishmen convinced. They got to cutting up and laughing with us. Tommy ran up to Mr. Law. He caught his tie in one hand and cut off the end of it with his knife.

"Here, Mr. Law, sir, I thought you might want this," said Tommy.

Everybody broke up laughing. Mr. Law looked at his tie, severed at one end and held the other ragged six inches in his hand.

"I say, old boy, I believe you cut my tie in two," he said. He paused a minute then added, "By God, that has never been done to me. Cut it."

From then on we got along real well and got into our recording. During that session we recorded "Osage Stomp," "Get With It," "Pray for the Lights to Go Out," "I Can't Give You Anything But Love," "Spanish Two-Step," "Maiden's Prayer," "Blue River," "Mexicali Rose," "I Ain't Got Nobody," "Never No Mo' Blues," "Who Walks In When I Walk Out?" "Old-Fashioned Love," "Oklahoma Rag," "Black and Blue Rag," "Sittin' on Top of the World," "Four or Five Times," and "I Can't Be Satisfied."

These were the first of 470 records that Bob was to make in his career. I made every one of the first 224 and I am damn proud of it.

The songs that Bob owned brought him quite a bit more money on royalties than ones that someone else owned. Due to this, and Bob's knack of thinking up melodies, and with all of the songs that had been in his family for several generations, and with some of us helping him with the arrangements and putting it on paper with the notes and chords for the copyrights, we spent a good deal of time getting ready for each recording session. But that was our job. We loved it.

I probably could write a book about each of our recordings. There was that much went on. None of them will I ever forget. But one that really stands out in my mind is the time we went to Chicago, for a recording session. It was on September 29 and 30, 1936, nearly one year exactly after that first session in Dallas.

Mr. Satherly and Mr. Law really fixed us up in style for that trip. They rented us a private railway car that was all our own. We were riding in style. High cotton is the way many of our fans would have put it.

There were thirteen musicians, Mr. Mayo and George the Hamburger King. He was not a musician, but Bob had invited him to go along. He was the only non-participant that ever made a recording trip with us. That gives you some idea of the high regard we all had for George the Hamburger King.

He was a native of Assyria. He was unmarried and lived alone in a little kind of a shack near his business in Bristow, Oklahoma, which was about forty miles west of Tulsa. That's how we met him. His business was a cafe. It was called "Hamburger King."

I don't believe I've ever eaten a better hamburger anywhere. He would pile them high with lettuce and tomatoes and onions and a chunk of meat that was so big you could stuff a cowboy boot full with it.

It got to be automatic to stop at his place. Not only did we enjoy eating there, but George was always so glad to see us. He would just bubble over with excitement and conversation.

"It's-a-been-so-a-long-since-I-a-seen-you-boy," he would say in his broken English. All of the time he would be getting his griddle hot and getting ready to cook us the damndest mess of hamburgers you've ever seen.

He never missed hearing one of our radio shows. And he came to see us play as often as he could. There was something else about George. He never would let us pay for our meals. He would get mad if we tried.

It finally got to the point that Bob told him that if he didn't start letting us pay, then we were going to stop coming to see him. He started letting us pay.

One time, Bob talked him into fixing us an Assyrian dinner. I don't have any idea what it consisted of. But it was good.

"Dis da vay ve fax 'em in da ol' coundry," he said.

George gave Bob a gorgeous diamond ring once. And

he gave him a saddle that was trimmed with silver. There was no telling how much that cost. He always gave us Christmas presents and seldom forgot any of our birthdays. That's why we felt proud to have George the Hamburger King with us on the train.

We arrived in Chicago on the morning of September 23. We were all dressed up in our western clothes and cowboy boots. We passed some waiting taxicabs. Some cabbies were grouped around talking. They looked at us. It was immediately apparent that we were not natives of Chicago. One of them said, "Hey, lookit them cowboys. Hey, cowboys. Where are your horses?"

Jesse Ashlock, who was a master at replying to such bullshit, said, "A jackass will do. Come on."

We checked into the old Jefferson Hotel. The next day we began recording. We rode to the studios in three cabs. The cabbie that I was riding with was named Potatoes.

"So you boys are from Oklahoma," he said. "Well, let me see, that is a long ways from here."

"You bet," I said.

He got more friendly, and before we got out he said, "If you boys need anything, I mean anything at all, you just take my number here and give me a call. Old Potatoes will be as ready to come as a bunch of french fries that's just been pulled from the skillet."

When we finished our work that afternoon, we called Potatoes and asked him to take us back to the hotel. He was all smiles again.

"You boys think you might like to see a special show tonight?" he said. "Probably not the kind you would see in Texas or Oklahoma. But it is free and I will take five of you out there and I can get one of my buddies to take the others who want to go."

He stabbed a Lucky Strike into his mouth and lighted it and continued, "I guarantee you will all be safe and if you don't enjoy this show, then your ride out there and back will be free."

That sounded like someone handing you a roll of toilet paper when there wasn't nothing but corncobs around. How could we lose. A free and special show with no strings attached.

"We're interested, Potatoes. We're interested," one of us said.

So that night all but two of us went with Potatoes and one of his buddies. Bob was one of the ones who didn't go. We were just as glad.

It took us about thirty minutes to get to the show. I have no idea of where it was. I had never been to a town the size of Chicago. All I know is that we went for miles in neighborhoods that had no street lights. By the time we got there we were scared. I mean really scared!

Potatoes finally stopped at an old run-down, two-story brick building that had a stairway going up the side. It was very dimly lit on the outside. Potatoes led us up the old wooden, rickety stairway, that groaned and creaked like an old man waking up in the morning after a bad night with rheumatism. He knocked at the door and finally a small crack appeared and someone said, "Who's there?"

"Just old Potatoes," he said, "and I got some friends from Oklahoma."

About this time I wasn't too sure about that friend business. I was thinking and hoping and wishing that I was back in Tulsa. One of the band members who had fortified himself rather well for the journey said, "Fellows, are we chicken or are we going to see this damn show that we drove all night to get to?"

It was like a football team kind of rallying to its leader. We got the fighting spirit. We all said, "Let's go gang!"

Potatoes left and said he would be back in two hours. That deflated our spirit all of a sudden. We felt like this might have been the end. I had that feeling. Because the person who had let us in that door was a great big, fat Negro. Her face looked like the hind flank of a rhinoceros.

And, just as tough. She looked like she might just smile us into the next world.

She led us into the parlor. I guess that's what it was. It was a big room, clean but old. It had old sofas and chairs. Over by a wall was a tall, old-fashioned phonograph. It was one of those you had to wind up by hand. She went over and put a real blues number on. This was the cue for a girl to appear. She did.

She was pretty and nicely dressed. For just a few minutes. Then she did some wiggly kind of moves that I never discovered at my senior proms and her clothes began coming off. The more she wiggled and the more she pulled off the quieter this bunch of Texas Playboys became. I don't know what the others were thinking. But I was thinking, "Man, if this is free, then maybe I might should move to friendly Chicago."

Finally, all of her clothes were off. She just kept on dancing and wiggling. The Playboys just kept on looking. Some were sweating. We all were thinking. And, it wasn't about music.

She left and another girl came out. She went through the same routine. I suddenly thought, "My God, here's another naked woman and the Texas Playboys haven't said anything. This just isn't like the Texas Playboys!"

The second girl left. The old record was still scratching out its music. Nobody was paying any attention to the scratches. We had other things to worry about. Then the old Smiling Rhino came back, smoothing out the wrinkles of her expansive, flowered dress. That's when we found out that not all things in life were free.

"Fellows, are you enjoying the show?" she asked. Nobody said anything. She went on. "The show is free, boys, but we do have some expenses and these two lovely ladies can do some private entertaining with you at a reasonable price. The first girl was Lilly and the second was Pearl. Now, tell me, who wants to be first?"

I had thought it was quiet when the dancing started.

But, it wasn't nearly so quiet as it was now. You could have heard a mouse sleeping on a pillow.

"Maybe you boys would like to see the girls again. Lilly. Pearl. Come on back in here," she said.

They came back. Both still naked, their black bodies looking like they had little diamonds sprinkled on them and the moon was catching their carats in its lights. But, still not a Playboy moved.

Then Smiling Rhino began playing her trump card. She said, "I was raised in the South. You know how neighbors help each other down there when they are in need. I remember one time when a man got sick just at cotton picking time and his neighbors all pitched in and picked all of his cotton and he never had to worry at all from his sickbed. That's kinda how it is with me. I've got some need and I figure you boys can help me. But, I'm not asking for something for nothing. For $25 I'll give you a special sex show . . . something that I'll damn near guarantee that you won't see in Oklahoma if you live to be a hundred and ten."

It wasn't that we wanted to see a sex show. But she had been nice to us. She had gone to a whole bunch of trouble for nothing so far. So we dug up the $25 and handed it to her.

"Thank you. Thank you kindly. Now if you will just follow me," she said, all of the time smiling.

Smiling Rhino showed us some sights that a bunch of old country boys had never seen. And, I'll tell you, before it was over none of us were smiling. And, by the time we left, Smiling Rhino wasn't smiling any more either because we had let her know that we hadn't appreciated the menu she had offered us.

We never told Bob about our activities. We knew he would be furious at us for getting into something like that. We also decided to not tell anyone about the trip. But, for years after that I would suddenly start thinking about

74

what had happened and wondered what we would have done if forty-six toughs had jumped from out of one of those darkened hallways and beaten us. We'd probably have never drawn another dime as musicians. Corpses just don't play very well.

Chicago was something else for us. You got to remember that we were just a bunch of old country boys. We plunged ourselves into its treasures, like kids finding a gallon bucket of Tootsie Rolls when their allowance was still a week away.

We ran into the city noises awed by the bumping and grinding and screeching and loud horns and noisy chatter of people, like a bunch of crows that have been locked up in a shoe box. We admired the tall buildings where we figured you could plant a different kind of crop on each floor, working your way up to the top and have plenty of floors left to plant the same crop several times.

We looked at the big lake, that breathed cold moisture onto our faces and made us wish that we had brought heavier clothing, but we had never expected anything like that in September. We went to the aquarium and listened as Mayo said, as he looked at a particularly big tank, "Gawd, how I'd like to set a trot line in there for about a couple of hours."

One day six or seven of us went walking on the beach of Lake Michigan. Bob had given us a few days to play around and we decided that beach would be a good place to do that.

The numbers we recorded while in Chicago that time were "She's Killing Me," "Weary of the Same Old Stuff," "No Matter How She Done It," "Bluin' the Blues," "Steel Guitar Rag," "Get Along Home Cindy," "Trouble in Mind," "What's the Matter with the Mill?" "Sugar Blues," "Basin Street Blues," "Red Hot Gal of Mine," "At the Darktown Strutter's Ball," "Too Busy," "Back Home Again in Indiana," "Fan It," "Mean Mama Blues," "Bring It on Down to My House," "Right or Wrong," "Swing Blues

75

Number One," "Swing Blues Number Two," and several others that were never released.

There was one really funny thing that happened during the recording sessions. Ray DeGear, a great sax and clarinet man, had been with us only a short time when we had that session. He came to us with excellent qualifications for a horn man. He had just come off of Red Nichols' band, which was one of the really big name bands of the day.

Ray, naturally, was not quite used to Bob's music and the way he put it on. He was used to cut and dried arrangements in which each member of the band only looked at those notes on the music under the reading lights. He had never seen people have to look at a leader all the time and constantly be ready for a break on their instrument.

Both his horns were B flat instruments, which meant that nearly all the music he had ever seen was written in the keys that would put him mostly in flats or at most, one or two sharps, like the key of G or D. Now when something was played in the key of E natural this would put him in six sharps or the key of F sharp.

Conventionally, no musician before Bob Wills put tunes in six sharps. But the famous "Steel Guitar Rag" was in the key of E natural. By the time we made this session in Chicago, the band had played several special arrangements with the horns and as we played the first four numbers in Chicago, Ray was doing great.

But, then came the fifth number. It was the "Steel Guitar Rag." As I have already said, Bob did all his arranging as he "felt it" while we were playing. And, never before had a sax played a chorus on "Steel Guitar Rag."

But, Bob felt that this was the time that a sax chorus would set the tune off. So he said, "Friends, here's Leon on the 'Steel Guitar Rag.' Take it away, Leon. Take it away."

Leon took it away as Bob "ahh-hahed" him on. Then he said, "Come on in, Al." After my piano chorus, there was some more from Leon, then Jesse on his fiddle chorus, some more Leon and then it happened. Bob said, "Now friends, here's Ray DeGear on that hot saxaphone."

Ray looked at Bob like he had just been hit in the face with a wet fish. He put the sax to his mouth and out came the wettest notes I ever heard in my life. He panicked. He started running scales trying to find the key. He finally gave up and shouted, "What the hell key is this in?"

The head honchos in the control room came storming out. They looked at Bob. Bob looked at Ray and said, "Man, I thought I had hired a great musician that could play anything, especially a simple thing like this number."

"Mr. Wills, I have always been able to play anything I was called on to play, but this is the first time I have ever seen a number in six sharps."

Bob knew as much about six sharps on a sax as I did about being the King of England.

"You can play what I want you to play or maybe this whole thing has been a mistake," said Bob.

Ray didn't say anything for a minute. He kept looking at his instrument and fingering it gently. Finally, he said, "Mr. Wills, if you will let me drink a couple of beers, I think I can satisfy you with a chorus on this song."

"Well, for God's sake, get this man some beer and let's get this show on the road," said Mr. Satherly.

Some beer was promptly brought to the studio. Ray uncapped a couple and chug-a-lugged them. We were all standing around and cheering him on. Finally the medicine began to take effect. But, Ray had one more request.

"Can I take off these Goddamn cowboy boots? They're killing me and I could concentrate much better if they were off," he said.

He was granted permission. He took them off, then picked up his sax and let me tell you something — if you have never heard the sax chorus that Ray DeGear played in Chicago on "Steel Guitar Rag" in six sharps you don't know what you've missed. It was sensational. The notes bounced to the top of the studio and then back down to the floor and we knew what we already knew. We had a helluva horn man in our midst.

We made another recording session in June, 1937. That one was in Dallas. We cut thirty numbers at the session but for some reason half of them were never released. The ones that were released were "White Heat," "Dedicated to You," "Playboy Stomp," "Steel Guitar Stomp," "Rosetta," "Bleeding Hearted Blues," "Tie Me to Your Apron String," "Never No More Hard Times Blues," "Sun Bonnet Sue," "New St. Louis Blues," "Loveless Love," and "Oozlin' Daddy Blues."

Many of these were good sellers. But, none of them were really among Bob's best sellers. I think "Rosetta" was the best one among that bunch. Bob did a beautiful job of singing that song.

Less than a year later we were back in Dallas again. That recording session in May saw us do several numbers. But, none were really big hits that came along later. "Loveless Love," was the best known song that we made that time.

But, six months later we went back to Dallas for another recording. And, that one produced the song that eventually made Bob famous. Besides me and Bob, there was Jesse, Sleepy, Tommy, Eldon, Joe, Leon, Johnnie Lee, Son Lansford, Zeb, Tiny Mott, Everett and Smokey.

I don't know, but it seemed like we were feeling real loose at that session, which took place on November 28, 29 and 30. Maybe it was that our stomachs were still full of Thanksgiving turkeys and pumpkin pies. I really can't say. But, there seemed to be a looseness among us like a kid who's fixing to go and play the lead in the senior play and he knows damn well in his heart that he's going to do a good job.

Our first number to record was, well, you guessed it, "San Antonio Rose." There's been a lot of stories told about "Rose." I hear new ones every day. But, since I was there, maybe I can get it straight.

Actually, one story that keeps popping up is that "San Antonio Rose," was really the "Spanish Two Step" played backwards. That's not right.

The "Spanish Two Step" was written by Bob while he was living in New Mexico and barbering and playing. There were a lot of Spanish people in the area and the tune has that tingling exuberance of Mexican music. You can almost imagine a bright cantina with hombres sitting around in their large sombreros drinking tequilla and shouting "ole" when you hear that.

The "Rose" was actually a modification of the "Two Step." It was rewritten a little and modified. Satherly named it.

When we made the first "Rose" it was just an instrumental. It featured Bob on his fiddle and Leon's steel guitar. That was it. The words to the new "San Antonio Rose" were still about seventeen months away.

The other numbers we recorded at this session were "Little Girl Go Ask Your Mamma," "Carolina in the Morning," "The Convict and the Rose," "Silver Bells," "Dreamy Eyes Waltz," "Beaumont Rag," "Twinkle Twinkle Little Star," "If I Could Bring Back My Buddy," "Whoa Babe," "Ida Red," "Yearning," "I Wonder If You Feel the Way I Do," "Prosperity Special," "Drunkard's Blues," "You're O.K.," "Liza Pull Down the Shades," "That's What I Like About the South," "My Window Faces the South," "The Waltz You Saved for Me," and "Don't Let the Deal Go Down."

The best sellers at that session were "The Convict and the Rose," "Ida Red," and "Silver Bells."

"San Antonio Rose" did okay. But, I must confess something. I just wasn't really that impressed with it. It was just another number to me. Boy was I ever in for a surprise. Because "San Antonio Rose" eventually was responsible for one of my greatest adventures with Bob Wills and His Texas Playboys.

FLEET OF BUICKS that Bob Wills bought to replace his first bus, 1937.

THE TEXAS PLAYBOYS "Big Band," complete with horn section, perform for KFJZ Radio Show in Fort Worth, 1940.

Chapter 8

W E WERE WEARING out sets of tires with all of the miles we were traveling across the country to make our appearances. We were wearing out strings on our instruments because they were being plunked so much. Somebody once said that he bet if he could tie all of the E strings from our guitars, fiddles and banjos and basses together that we wore out, he could build him a wire fence that would easily surround a four-section ranch.

Our records were being played on every little jukebox in every little greasy spoon cafe. And, some of them big fancy dude restaurants in Tulsa even had our music on them. We were like someone who has discovered a giant oak bee tree and has plunged his hands down into the honey inside the trunk and drawed it out and started licking his fingers. We were doing some good licking. But, we faced some more trouble.

That came from the musicians' union. It happened soon after the band started playing in and out of Tulsa. The musicians' union seemed most disturbed that a hill-billy band was horning in on their territory. They got more disturbed as our crowds grew and grew.

Finally, the union began raising a fuss. We called them

legit musicians. They were mad, they said, because we were not members of the union.

Bob offered to make them happy. He said he would pay dues for all of the boys and would also pay the regular fees. They refused our offer. The board of the union ruled that we were not good enough to qualify as musicians.

They seemed to feel that anyone who could not read music could not rightfully belong to their union. So Bob just went on playing and minding his own business. He had made his offer. He had been turned down. So to hell with them.

But the union did not let it stop there. What happened will always leave a sore spot with me. We discovered it one night when we were playing at Tulsa. There were a bunch of men standing outside. They had picket signs in their hands.

"What the hell is going on?" someone asked.

"We're being picketed. It's as simple as that," said Smokey.

We crossed the picket line and played anyway. Lots of people kept coming to our dances. They thought the pickets were ridiculous. So they crossed the lines, too. As a result, some of them were fined.

But, in spite of all of this, the crowds kept growing. And, sometimes, the picketers themselves would become disgusted with their duties. I remember one night, shortly after we had started playing, there was a commotion at the front. Some of the picketers were coming in. Without their signs. One of them said, "Hell, this is ridiculous. To set out there with a damn picket sign when this good music is being played inside."

He and several others had come on in and listened to us play.

But, finally, the union took another tack. They kept track of the crowds. They were no fools. They knew we were drawing thousands. So they figured it was more important to get some revenue from the Texas Playboys than to worry about some rule that said how good a guy should be on a certain instrument. That's how, in 1935, Bob Wills and His Texas Playboys became union musicians.

But, the union was totally unforgiving. One night at Fort Smith, we played at the Winter Garden. When we left, our bus was out of gas. There was an all-night station across the street. We didn't know there was another station open at that hour. So we filled up our bus at that station.

The only thing wrong was that this station was a Diamond X station. The refinery that furnished the gas for the station was Mid-Continent in Tulsa. That refinery was on strike. But, we didn't know that when we gassed up.

We all felt that in a case like that, we would be in the clear to buy gas from the station, particularly since we had not seen any pickets around. But, a week later Bob got a letter. It was a notice that he was being fined for buying from an unfair station.

He tried to explain. But it did no good. He finally had to pay the $75 fine. That was just one of the little ways the union tried to irritate Bob or make him feel that someone had tiptoed silently into his room at night and sprinkled some grassburrs in his underwear.

Eventually, reading music did catch up with the band. Our competition was growing. We had to grow too. So Bob added some fine horn men to the band. That made it very difficult for some of us who were just so-so in reading music.

Bob called a meeting one day. It was serious. You could tell by the look on his face. It looked like a tractor tire had run through some soft dirt. That's how many wrinkles were there.

"Boys, I'm having to go up and up and this means putting some musicians in the band who can read music. I hate to say this, but if you can't cut it this new way, I've got no choice. I'm going to have to replace you," he said.

This may sound tough. But it was plain that in order

to meet his obligation and competition, Bob was going to have to do this.

One of the first men Bob ever hired was given the job of driving the bus and taking tickets at the door. Others were farmed out to some other band. One of Bob's brothers had a band and some were sent to him. And, then there was me. I was scared to death. I was like the kid who got a whipping at school and hadn't told his daddy about it and then there comes a knock at the door after dark and that kid is almost certain that it's the principal coming to tell his dad what a sorry son he has.

I had taught piano before coming to Bob, but I knew very little about reading music. All of my students had been taught my way. That was playing by ear. But I knew I was going to have to change.

I managed pretty well until we got a new arrangement. It was "Beat Me Daddy, Eight to the Bar." This was a new kind of beat that Tommy Dorsey had inserted into this arrangement. The left hand had to hit eight beats to a measure or bar.

Up until this time, I had played what was called a two-four beat with my left hand. In other words a bass and a chord in that order, and only four beats to a bar. To double up and play eight beats to a bar, was to me, just about impossible. It would be like telling an old country boy to go up and make love to some movie star. He'd go up and ask and then just wait for the explosion.

I never told Bob about my problem. I was afraid that I'd become another driver or ticket taker or commode swabber.

We didn't play that "daddy" business for about a couple of weeks. I'll bet that I worked on that thing at least two hundred hours. I would do it over and over and over. It still didn't sound right. I just couldn't make that left hand go. But, I finally played it for Bob. He came over afterwards. I just knew he was going to say, "Al, I need a good bus driver." He didn't. "Al, you did great," he said.

I may have. But I never learned to like Tommy Dorsey's "Beat Me Daddy, Eight to the Bar." And, I'd still feel that way even if I were to win a contest at Carnegie Hall playing the damn thing.

There was another difficult number for me. That was "One O'Clock Jump." The introduction had sixteen bars of an introduction with just the piano and drums. Count Basie, a great pianist, had composed this thing. He could play the hell out of a piano, especially this arrangment. Here I was supposed to play it note for note just like he did.

I worked my tail off on that one too. Hundreds of hours were spent working on it. Practicing it. Perfecting it. Dreaming about it. Nightmares, they were. I finally got it down pretty good, or so I thought, on the piano.

It was about this time that we had to make out our radio program two weeks in advance because of some kind of mix-up between composer associations. One day the big day arrived. I was to play "One O'Clock Jump." It happened on the day we were doing our radio show from Bixby, Oklahoma, a little town south of Tulsa. They were having an annual celebration and they asked Bob to do his noon show from there.

It sounded like a fun occasion. It should have been. There was just one problem for me. The good people of Bixby did not have a piano available. So they put an old pump organ up on the truck bed that was to be used for our bandstand.

As the time approached for us to play our first number, Everett Stover leaned over and said, "Al, baby, do you know that the first number on the program is going to be 'One O'Clock Jump?'"

"Huh?" I said. I felt like jumping up and crying. The only time I have ever been more frightened was when I was a participant in a wild car race and I was riding with Johnnie Lee Wills.

I got to thinking that it would have been much better

if I had never been born. Then I got to thinking that maybe lightning would flash down from the sky and knock me unconscious and when I woke up the show would all be over and everyone would be happy that I hadn't been killed. There were two problems. There were no clouds in the sky and I'd never seen it lightning when there weren't no clouds. The other problem was the show was just about to begin.

There wasn't a damn thing to do. The show had been made out two weeks previous and it had to go just like it was. I was going to have to play that fast, difficult number on a pump organ, when I would be doing well to play it on a twelve-foot grand piano.

When I play, I stomp both feet to the rhythm of the music. I can't hit a damn note if I can't stomp my feet. In fact, it would be so bad when we made records, they had to put rags under my feet to keep me from out-drumming the drums.

We went on the air with our theme song. Then Everett Stover said, "Ladies and gentlemen out there in radio land, we bring you as our first number today, Count Basie's fast and furious 'One O'Clock Jump,' a novel tune, featuring Al Stricklin at the piano with Smokey Dacus at the drums."

He paused, then added, "Wait a minute. It is Al Stricklin at the pump organ . . . GEEZ!"

Everett gave us the downbeat. I was sweating profusely. I mean like a preacher who has done been caught with one of the deacon's daughters out in the hayloft. But, I began. I was making the damndest racket you ever heard in your life.

"Squeak, squeak, squak. Squeak, squak, squeak, squeak."

Smokey was flailing those drums like crazy and I was squaking with all my might. You had to pump the organ with both feet and since I am such a foot patter anyway, I was pumping away like I was trying to win a bicycle race, stomping and kawhomping and all of the time being scared out of my hide.

After the sixteen bars, which it seemed like it took hours

to get through, the horns were supposed to pick the damn thing up. They didn't. The guys were all so tickled they couldn't pucker into their mouthpieces. They just left it with Smokey and me. It seemed like an eternity. I swear my life passed in front of my eyes ninety-two times and at the end of each time, it was featuring me back in Fort Worth sweeping floors. But finally, it ended. Believe me, for the life of me, I can't remember how it ended.

Everyone was cracking up. They kept laughing and laughing. Finally they quit and the show went on. I'd like to go back to Bixby some day just to see if I could relax there. But I doubt it, because I still dream about that day and in some of those dreams, this pump organ has suddenly become an ugly giant musical instrument with big hands and is beating the hell out of me because I've been stomping on its toes so much.

We were playing at some places where some of the big-name bands like Paul Whiteman, Tommy Dorsey and Woody Herman were playing. We outdrew them by a big margin. One man learned that the expensive way when he booked us to play in a place in Kansas where we'd never played before.

He asked Mr. Mayo how much he wanted. Mayo told him $2000 for one night.

"Jesus Christ, man, I can get any band in the country for that price," said the man.

"Well just go right ahead and get them, then," said Mayo. "You are the one who called."

The man asked if we would play for commission.

"Fine, we'd rather work any place on commission than guarantee. We'll play for 65 percent of the gate," said Mayo.

The man hired us. He was elated because he thought nobody was going to have that many people. So we went up and played. When it was over, the man counted out nearly $800 more than the guarantee price Mayo had asked him. The man was sick because $800 in those days was lots of money.

"I was a fool," he muttered as we were leaving.

We got into trouble occasionally with our bookings. That occurred when we played a first in a place in Missouri. As usual, we had a signed contract between the manager there and Mr. Mayo, with Bob's signature and approval.

Bob got sick right before the dance and couldn't make it. At times like this it was a bit rough because people came out to hear Bob Wills. When he wasn't there, especially at a place for the first time, they became unhappy. But we went ahead and played.

Tommy, who fronted the band when Bob wasn't there, had a rough time that night. It came in the form of a drunk woman. She stood right in front of the bandstand all night. Every five minutes she would pull Tommy's pants leg and say, "Whersh Bob Willish?"

At first Tommy would say that Bob would be along later. But, as the night went along, it became apparent that Bob was not going to be there. So Tommy started telling the folks that Bob was sick and couldn't make it.

Mayo was watching all of this. He suggested that we make an announcement that if anyone was not having a good time and wanted their money back, they could come to the front door and he would cheerfully refund their money. Nobody left.

About 11:30 P.M., this pesky woman grabbed the mike stand and pulled the mike down. She started screaming into it. Her voice was slurred as she said, "Bob Wills and His Texas Playboys . . . without Bob Wills, the Playboys are hog slop."

We went on and finished the job. While we were packing our equipment, Mayo settled with the owner. He came to the bus.

"Boys, we had a big crowd — a big money crowd. But, we never got paid a dime. Even though the people seemed contented, the man said the crowd was disappointed and this situation might ruin his crowd in the future on account of 'false advertising.' "

He also claimed, said Mayo, that the contract was with Bob Wills and the boys. Without him, it was a complete breach of contract. I always thought that guy was a first class sonofabitch.

But there were plenty of those around. Some of them showed up in the band sometimes. They would get to thinking they could do anything that Bob Wills could do.

And, finally, they would start saying, "We do all the work and Bob gets all of the money. I feel like I could get a band and be just as successful and make the kind of money I deserve."

Bob had a unique way of handling this. I remember one guy who started this routine and Bob asked him to ride to an engagement with him in his car. During the 140-mile ride, Bob started talking to the fellow.

"I've been thinking lately about the talent you have and have been wondering why you don't try it on your own. Now don't misunderstand me, I am not trying to get rid of you. It's just that you need to try it now if you ever intend to," said Bob.

He said he could help him get a band down in Texas and a sponsor for radio. He even said that he would give him a bus.

The griper acted like Bob had read his mind. He could hardly contain himself. He thought Bob was being very generous. The truth was that Bob wanted him to find out just how cruel the world was out there.

This guy left. He flopped. It didn't take long. He went broke. He wound up back in Tulsa. When Bob heard he was back, he made some adjustments in his band to make room for him and let him play with us again. The guy was really happy.

Bob said later, "I knew he'd be back. He does get foolish sometimes. But he's a helluva musician."

As our fame spread, we started getting a steady stream of people who wanted to audition for our band. I'm sure that happens to all good bands. Bob went out of his way to be nice to these people. It kinda worked a hardship on me. Because I had to listen to them as they sawed or hammered away at whatever instrument they were supposed to be good on. I must have listened to hundreds play so I could recommend them to Bob if he ever found a need for any of them.

It got pretty boring. But it was frightening too. Particularly giving a piano player an audition. That was the hardest part for me, because I naturally had an inferiority complex anyway. But I know I had many piano players come and audition who were better than me.

Several times I would tell Bob that.

"That guy can play rings around me, Bob. Why don't you put him on?" I said many times. Bob would just smile.

"Al, you are my piano player as long as you want to be. They haven't made the guy who can take your place," he always said.

Another job I had was to try out the songs that the hundreds of song writers sent us. Believe me, everybody and their dog sent us songs. Bob told me to try every one that came in. If one had merit, I was supposed to bring it to the attention of the band, and we would give it a good trial.

Out of those hundreds, about ten or twelve made it to the bandstand. Out of that number, there were probably only two or three that we ever used.

People used to try and hire me to play their songs. They would want me to put their bungled notes into music. These things would be like trying to untwist the wire from four hundred bales of hay.

I finally solved that problem. I put my price so high that people couldn't afford to hire me. Hell, if I were going to write songs, I would do it for myself and not somebody else.

There was another thing that began happening regularly as a result of us becoming so well known. People got to saying that they knew us back when or that they were kin to us. Or that they went to school with us.

Bob once said that people who claimed they went to school with him numbered in the hundreds. What makes that so ridiculous is that Bob went all his school years to a small school out in the country near Turkey, Texas. There were only about fifty kids in the whole school during Bob's seven years of schooling.

The same thing happened to me one time. It was about 1938. I was taking a short vacation and doing some running around with my brother in Texas. We were driving to a little town west of Fort Worth. We picked up a nice young man hitchhiking.

"What do you guys do for a living?" he asked.

"I'm a newspaper writer and my brother is a musician," said my brother.

What this hitchhiker said next nearly floored us. He said, "I am a musician and I have just recently been playing with Bob Wills up in Oklahoma."

"Really," I said. "What do you play?"

"Oh, I play the piano. I'm sure you've heard of me. I'm old Al Stricklin," he said.

At first I thought he was being funny. He wasn't. He was telling this for the truth. Somehow, my brother and I kept straight faces. After about twenty minutes, we let the kid out. As he was leaving, he said, "By the way, I didn't get your names."

I took out my union card, which had my name and Tulsa, Oklahoma written on it. I handed it to him to look at. He read my card, swallowed his adam's apple, turned and took off in a fast run.

We both laughed and my brother said, "Al, I didn't know you were so famous. And I never thought I'd see the day when I'd be around and someone would say that he was Al Stricklin."

I must admit, I didn't either. It was the Bob Wills' magic. And I loved it!

Chapter 9

ANYONE ALIVE TODAY who was alive in the 1930s can tell you times were rough. Groceries were hard to come by. So you often just ate the cheapest food there was around. That's where pinto beans came in right handy. Thank God for the great pinto.

Many a family was saved during these times by the cheap price of the pinto bean. They were high in protein and they stuck to your ribs.

We were making pretty good money. We were in better shape than most of the people were during those days. But, many times when we'd go into a cafe to eat during our road trips, some of the boys would order something like a chicken fried steak and then say, "By the way, if that's a pot of pintos I smell cooking back in the kitchen, would you put me a couple of good dips of them on my plate?"

We did a lot of things to pass time while we were driving to our dances. We invented a lot of little games. One was a spelling match. We would choose up sides and somebody would give out words from a newspaper or a book. Son Lansford was the best speller.

Another game we played involved counting livestock. We just counted cattle and horses and mules. In this game,

TEXAS PLAYBOYS perform for Texarkana Radio KCMC in 1938 with Gene Autry.

O. W. MAYO, the business manager of the band. Al said "We couldn't have done without him."

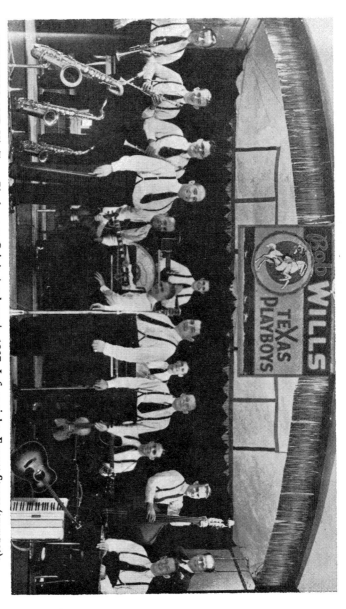

BOB WILLS AND His Texas Playboys at Cain's Academy in 1937. Left to right: Everett Stover (trumpet); Ray Degere (sax and clarinet); Zeb McNally (sax and clarinet); Bob Wills (leader and fiddle); Herman Arnspiger (guitar); Smokey Dacus (drums); Al Stricklin (piano); Tommy Duncan (vocalist); Johnnie Lee Wills (banjo); Jesse Ashlock (fiddle); Sleepy Johnson (guitar); Joe Ferguson (bass); Leon McAuliffe (steel guitar); O. W. Mayo (business manager).

we would set a limit, say of thirty miles. The side with the most animals won.

We had our own rules. Like if you saw a white horse on your side, it canceled out your total and you had to start over. But, if you sa wa cemetery on your side, it doubled your total. We got into some pretty heated arguments sometimes. Like the time someone said he saw a white horse on the other person's side.

"You've got to start over," he hollered.

"Hell, that wasn't a white horse. That was a grey horse just standing in the shade and you thought he was white," said the other party.

Another game we played was like poker. We'd use the numbers on license tags of cars for cards. Four of us played at a time. Each would get a car or truck that we met. If the license on your vehicle had two ones, that meant you had a pair of aces. It worked like stud poker.

Those may sound like childish games. But, you consider we were traveling better than 30,000 miles a year and most of that by bus, and anything that helped the miles float by was welcomed.

Much as I hated riding the bus, there were times when I wished I was on it. That happened once in 1936 when Johnnie Lee bought a new Terraplane and Son Lansford bought a new Chevy. Since these guys were cousins, the inevitable happened. They got to arguing which car was the fastest. We all knew it was just a matter of time before they had a race.

It finally happened one night when we were playing in Okmulgee, about thirty-eight miles from Tulsa. I rode with Johnnie Lee in his Terraplane that night. When we pulled into the parking lot, there was Son stepping out of his new Chevy. He had a grin on his face.

"Wait until the dance is over, Johnnie Lee, and we are going to see who's got the fastest car. That is if you ain't afraid to accept a challenge," said Son.

"I'll suck you up in my exhaust pipes. This Terraplane

just loves to eat Chevys for midnight snacks," said Johnnie Lee.

The challenge had been accepted. All through that dance, I was worrying. I kept missing some beats because I kept thinking about those hairpin curves and I could just see myself lying all tangled up in the twisted wreckage of that Terraplane when it hadn't made the curve. I felt like I had been condemned to die.

After the dance, I thought about telling Johnnie Lee that I had a bad case of the GI trots and I couldn't ride with him because if I did, he'd have to be stopping all of the time to let me run to the bushes and I'd be responsible for him losing the race and I didn't want that to happen and . . . I went ahead and got into the car with him. He gunned the engine up real loud and it was squawling like a cow that's been hit with a cattle prod. Son was warming his Chevy up. It sounded the same way. The race was on.

Son would get a little ahead on the straightaways and Johnnie Lee would pass him on the curves. We hadn't gone but a few miles and all of us were begging him to stop. He thought that was funny and he just kept laying his feet onto that accelerator. If he had had longer toes, he'd probably have stopped up the carburetor.

"I'll give you my house. My car. My wife . . . anything, if you'll just stop," I pleaded. He just grinned and swamped around another curve, hitting gravel and sending it showering over into the bar ditch. He let loose with another loud stream of laughter and kept at it.

We made thirty-eight miles in about twenty-nine minutes. That might not sound fast today. But, if you know anything about how the roads were in Oklahoma back then, you'd think that was impossible. Johnnie Lee won the race, but he lost some future passengers.

I remember getting out and kissing the ground. Johnnie Lee just kept on grinning. He said, "You boys can thank me for getting you home so quickly. You can get more sleep tonight."

"You can get you some new seats," said Sleepy, who had been riding with us.

"What do you mean, Sleepy?" asked Johnnie Lee.

"You go over there and look where I was sitting and you'll see that my butt ate holes in that seat," said Sleepy.

That was one night when his name was a misnomer, to be sure. He sure as hell wasn't sleeping on that ride. That would have been impossible. The squawling of the tires would have kept anyone awake.

That was a wild story. And it was true. But I've heard lots of wild stories about the Texas Playboys that weren't true. One that kept cropping up was about our drinking. Some people said that we were drunk all the time. I think those opinions probably came because we exhibited so much life and enthusiasm. Some people thought we had to be drunk to act that way.

But, really, though we certainly weren't Sunday School teachers, you could count on the fingers of one hand the number of boys that ever got on the bandstand drunk. It still makes me mad today when I hear someone say, "Yeah, I was at a Bob Wills' dance once, and he and the whole bunch were so drunk they could hardly stand up." That just didn't happen. Even the ones with drinking problems, and some of them definitely had them, were never permitted on the bandstand when they were drunk.

However, I do remember one night when that wasn't exactly true. Son took his Chevrolet to Fayetteville and asked me and Leon and Smokey to ride with him. If you put all the whiskey from every drink this crew had while they were with the band, a child could carry the container. We all were almost teetotalers.

On this trip, however, we had been hearing about some wine that someone had recommended highly to us. They had said, "It tastes like Kool-Aid going down. It's sure good."

So we decided to stop and get us some of the Kool-Aid. I'll never forget the name. It was Nelson's Port. We bought

94

five gallons. We thought we would just keep it around for holidays and things.

We got there way ahead of time, since Son was such a fast driver. That Chevrolet would run. Someone suggested, while we were waiting, that maybe we should taste that wine. We opened up a jug and passed it around for awhile. By the time the dance started, we were on the second jug.

That Nelson's had a hypnotic power to it. Because all during the dance, we kept sneaking out and trying some more of it. And, after the dance, we decided that Nelson's was better than food, and we kept at it. By the time it was time to go home, we got to arguing about who was going to drive.

"Al's the sosberish, so let him drive," said Leon.

I wasn't exactly sober. I probably would have taken a bear on with a flyswatter. The bear would have clobbered me, I'm sure. But I'll bet I'd have swore that I won.

Smokey rode in the front to keep me awake. It was about 135 miles to Tulsa. We started out frisky. Everyone was singing and carrying on. But, after about twenty miles, I was the only one awake. The rest had crapped out. I should have pulled over and done likewise. I didn't.

I came to a detour. While trying to negotiate it, I turned at the wrong place. I detoured off the detour. The moon was out, a big fat pulsating yellow, hanging up in the sky. All I could see ahead were miles and miles of dirt roads.

I kept driving. And driving, and driving. I had no idea of where I was. I just knew I was driving. Finally, just as the sun was coming up, Smokey raised his head up and asked where we were.

"Hell, I have no idea, Smokey," I said. "I just think we are somewhere in Oklahoma."

We finally got to a paved road. I thought it would be smart to head away from the rising sun. I did. Soon I came to a black guy who was hitchhiking. I picked him up.

He was wearing a straw hat and overalls. He had a big smile and seemed friendly. I asked, "Friend, do you have any idea of where Tulsa is?"

"Naw, sir, I've never been there, but I know it's a far piece from here," he said.

Some of the others had woke up. We told him who we were.

"You boys shore nuff are Bob Wills' Texas Playboys? I listen to you all the time. All I can tell you is that you's a long ways from home," he said.

We finally got to a small town. There was a service station there and we stopped for gas. The old man who was running it said, "You boys are about 200 miles from Tulsa."

He started laughing when we told him where we'd come from. "You sure got your asses lost," he said. We sped away, leaving his laughter behind.

We were worrying about two things now. One was our wives. The other was making the 12:30 broadcast on time. Everyone was awake but Son. Old Nelson still had him in a stranglehold.

We roared into Tulsa about 11:30 A.M. I let Leon out first and then took Smokey home. His wife was waiting. She didn't look too happy.

I took Son home. His wife wasn't happy either. We couldn't get Son awake. She really was unhappy then.

All but Son made it to the broadcast. Bob looked us over and said, "You all look like you sure got a good night's sleep."

He found out later what had happened. He always found out. But he didn't say anything.

We had another similar trip one time when we went to Dallas to play a job. We left on Sunday. We were in our fleet of Buicks.

Tommy was driving the car that I was in. One of the boys had a road map and he was going to show us a short cut to Dallas. The last familiar town we passed was Ada. We drove and drove. Finally someone said, "By gawd, this doesn't look too familiar to me."

It was getting dark and it started to rain. Seemed like

it rained for hours. Tommy had to slow down to about fifteen miles per hour. Finally, we saw some lights and a sign.

"Boys, I've found something," said Tommy. He got out in the downpour with a flashlight. He got back into the car. He said, "Boys, we are in Scullin, Oklahoma."

"How big is it?" I asked.

"Population two," said Tommy. "That's what the sign said."

I thought he was putting us on. I got out and checked. He wasn't putting us on.

About this time, one of the group who was a hard drinker said he really needed a drink. He had run out of whiskey and he had the shakes. He kept pleading with us to stop and let him buy a bottle. It seemed ridiculous to stop in a place with a population of two, so we kept driving in the rain.

We finally came to another light and this guy talked us into stopping. He went up there. He came back. He was soaked. He said, "I knocked and knocked on this door, and finally this man came and I asked him who could sell me some whiskey. He said, 'You won't find any here, brother. This is the house of God.'"

We all died laughing. He had gone to a church to ask for whiskey.

Of course, I'm sure a lot of people have heard about Bob's drinking. I won't say too much about this. But he wasn't a Sunday School teacher either. I do remember one time he got a little tight.

He was staying in a motel and it was after a dance. He had retired to his room to try to salve some of the irritations of the day. He had taken a bottle with him.

For some reason, he had to leave in a hurry. We called his room and said he had to go. Someone went in there to wake him up. Bob was in such bad shape that they had to try and dress him. He kept mumbling something as the dressing went on. He really got to mumbling when they got to his boots and were trying to help him put them on. The boots just wouldn't go on.

"Goddamn, Bob, you need to get you some new boots. These damn things just don't fit you," said one of the band members who was working with him. He kept trying to push the boots on Bob. Bob kept mumbling.

"Damn, Bob, it's no wonder you are after our asses sometimes. Putting these boots on would try the patience of a Catholic sister," said the band member.

He still couldn't get them on. All the time, Bob was mumbling. Finally, it dawned on the guy what Bob was trying to say. He was saying, "Shouchs. Shouchs. Dammit, them shouchs."

What he was trying to say was, "Socks. Socks."

Bob had his socks in the boots. That's why the fellow couldn't get the boots on. There's no way you can cram anyone's feet into a pair of cowboy boots if the socks are still in there. Not even the best damn fiddle player in the world.

But we loved Bob. We loved him for many reasons. One was the fact that he was the reason we were getting to have all of these adventures that we were having. But there were other reasons. One was that Bob treated us like humans. Like men. He never treated us differently.

I remember one time Bob got sick. He was ill for about two weeks. At the same time, there was a long, cold, icy stretch of weather. We learned then, as we did many times, that people were coming to the dances to see Bob Wills and His Texas Playboys. Not just the Texas Playboys.

We were not drawing good crowds. The weather was bad. Our bus started giving trouble. Even for those days, the payroll was a pretty tidy little sum. So here we had all of these bad things going and all of this money going out and . . . well, it was bound to catch up with the bank account sooner or later. It did.

Bob could have said he was sorry and let it go at that. But he didn't. He cashed in some of his insurance policies

98

so he could keep our paychecks coming. They kept coming.

I'm convinced that Bob would have kept our paychecks coming even if it had meant him selling his furniture or something. He was that kind of guy. He believed a deal was a deal and he kept his word on it, even though it might have meant some hardships for him.

Sometimes when money would get a little short, Bob would book a few of those school shows on the way to a dance. Then maybe we would play a Sunday show some place. We'd pick up several hundred dollars and everyone would keep getting paid.

I remember one time thinking about all of that. It hit me then why Bob did it. I mean, why he tried to take care of his band. He looked on us as humans, as I've said. And, he had been raised in that rugged old West Texas country that treated its residents savagely sometimes. He knew what it was like to go hungry. He knew it hurt you inside. Not only physically, but mentally. He didn't ever want our band to feel that way. He wanted us to look and be proud. And by God, we always did. Even when the Nelson's Port got a little heavy in our guts.

Chapter 10

I KEEP HEARING people talking about the good old days. Often those good old days were the 1930s when I was playing with Bob. I guess they were good old days.

Beef was selling for nine dollars a hundred. That was fat beef, too, that had been on feed for several months. You could buy a complete set of false teeth for thirty-five dollars. I remember reading one ad that said that. It went on to say, "They are built to suit your own facial looks. Even your uncle won't know that you're wearing them when he talks to you up close."

There were a lot of people who thought being a Texas Playboy would be the best way to live in them good old days. A lot of them auditioned for us, as I've already noted.

Taking it all the way around, I mean as far as instruments were concerned, I think Leon and his steel guitar had to be the most popular instrument in our band. Bob worked it perfectly. Leon loved it. As a result of Bob's famous "Take it away, Leon" and Leon's equally famous playing the hell out of that steel guitar, there were hundreds of kids wanting to learn to play the steel guitar. I remember standing around one day listening to a kid audition with a steel guitar. When he finished, I thought he sounded

100

like two cats that had been high lifed and put inside a rusty barrel. I asked him as he was leaving why he was learning to play the steel guitar (and believe me he was learning). He stood up tall and said, "I want to play it the way Take-it-away-Leon McAuliffe does."

One time about fifteen minutes before our radio show, we got a request for an unusual audition. About a dozen people came up and asked if their little girl could play the radio show with us. Bob always gave everybody a chance, if he could. But, this seemed a bit too much.

"Tell you what folks," he said, tilting his big white hat back on his head. (You could see some sweat popping out and you knew that Bob didn't want to hurt these people's feelings.) "Why don't we audition her first and then maybe sometime in the future we can put her on?"

"Okay," said the father. "We understand. We'll bring her back sometime."

They started out. Bob looked out and he saw only one child with them. He really pushed his hat back then. The girl had no arms. She just had shoulders. Absolutely no arms.

"Go get them folks and bring them back," he said.

One of us stopped the people and brought them back. Bob was looking at the little girl. He began talking, his voice deep with emotion. He said, "Is this the little lady that plays the steel?"

"Yes, sir, Mr. Wills, this is her," said the mother.

Bob reached down and put his arm around the little girl and hugged her. He said, "Honey, you can play on my radio show anytime you want."

I know that Bob was being kind and generous. I felt good that he was. But, I know, and I figured the rest of the band felt the same way, and probably Bob did too, that this little girl could no more play the steel guitar than I could be the pope. And there was no way I could be the pope. I'm not even Catholic. But, there are other reasons too.

101

But, we helped this little girl get her steel guitar set up. The band tuned our instruments so we were all together. Then the show began. We played a couple of numbers. All of us kept wondering what was going to happen and how Bob was going to introduce this little girl. He finally did. He said, "Friends out there in radio land, we've got a beautiful little lady who is with us today. She's going to entertain you now. She is going to play the steel guitar."

Let me tell you. She surprised everyone. She cut loose on the "Steel Guitar Rag." She played the hell out of it. She played it much like Leon did and never lost time or music. She did that with her toes. She used those toes like we use our fingers. She was an instant hit. Not only with the band, but with the fans.

After the show, I went up to her and said, "Sweetheart, you can play with me anytime."

"Make that 'us' anytime," said Bob.

She just grinned widely, then played with us some more. We kept up with her for a long time. I don't know what ever happened to her, but I'll bet she was a success. She made her own dresses, cooked and combed her hair. She did it all, just like she played that steel. Like a professional.

Really, I wasn't surprised when Bob let that girl play on the show. That was in his nature. It was carved into his being. He'd have let that girl play even if she had struck notes that would have made a church choir frown. He just loved people!

When we were out on the road or at dances, people would write down requests for Bob to play on his radio program the next day. Bob never overlooked a request. He gave me the responsibility of writing down the requests.

"Al, don't you ever throw them away. There's people out there depending on us for these," he told me. I never threw them away.

Many of these requests would be for old people, or shut-ins, or people who were sick. It meant a lot to Bob to help these people. He'd always make it a point to say something nice to them before the request. I always figured that part of his wanting to do that might have gone back to the days when he was thinking about being a preacher and he figured this was his own kind of missionary work.

That's what caused him on many occasions to take off in the daytime, when he was tired and desperately needed some rest, and go and sing at someone's funeral or visit a shut-in or help some relative or friend. He was eager to do this.

I remember one woman who lived in a nursing home out from Tulsa. She was a daily listener to Bob's show. She asked Bob to play her a tune on his fiddle one day. That day was her one hundred and twelfth birthday. We played the song. Then Bob said, "Lady, we are going to come out to your party. You must be a real sweet person and I have just got to have a piece of your cake."

Bob didn't go by himself. The whole band went. We played a concert for this woman and the other folks there. The audience had tears in their eyes when we were through. We all walked out and started talking to them. One grabbed Bob's hand, her fingers wrinkled and with veins that stood out like long pieces of spaghetti. She said, "God bless you, Mr. Wills. Mr. Bob Wills, God bless you!"

The old lady who was having the party was blind. But she could hear. Her face broke out in a wide smile. As the music went along, she would let out with little hollers.

"I may be too old to dance to the music, but I'm not too old to appreciate it," she said.

She died about a year after that. We went to her funeral. Bob played. As usual, there were about six of us who went to these. Bob always played one special song. It was "There Is No Disappointment in Heaven." He not only played it, he sang it. And, how he could sing that song!

He had a fine, clear voice that enunciated every word. You could almost see water pouring clear and pure from one of those old windmills out on the wind-battered West Texas landscapes as he sang. The words went:

There is no disappointment in Heaven.
No weariness, sorrow or pain.
No hearts that are bleeding or broken.
No song with a minor refrain.
No clouds of the earthly horizon
Will ever appear in the sky.
Where all will be sunshine and gladness
With never a sob nor a sigh.
I'm bound for that beautiful city
Our Lord has prepared for His own.
Where all the redeemed of all ages
Sing glory around the white throne.
Sometimes I grow homesick for Heaven
And, the joys my eyes shall behold.
Oh, what joy that will be when my Savior I see,
In that beautiful City of Gold.

That song was beautiful. But Bob would sing or play any song that was requested of him. It didn't make any difference who the request was for or from. Even people in prison. Bob played for them. He felt close to these men. One time we went to the state prison at McAlester, Oklahoma and played for the inmates. The warden had invited us. But, I'm sure it was Bob's missionary desires that were as responsible for us being there as the warden's invitation.

We played our noon broadcast from the men's dining room. You talk about applause. I've never heard anything like it. It sounded like someone firing shotgun blasts from inside a concrete culvert.

"These boys like you," said the warden. "They listen to you every day while they're eating dinner. That's probably why they're applauding so much. Here you are right up in front of them."

That probably was right. But I think it was Bob's appeal that turned them on so much. His music did everyone that way. I've often thought, and many more people back me up on this thinking, that Bob, having once been a servant of the land, put the land and life into his music. That's why the people loved it. That's why the convicts went so wild.

We were taken on a guided tour of the prison. We visited the shops and working areas. We visited death row. We met a young man who was really nice to us. He talked and said, "Man, I really like your music. It makes me glad I'm alive."

He wouldn't be alive long. He was to be executed in the electric chair in forty-eight hours.

The prison band played for us. They were really good. We reciprocated the applause they had given us earlier. Then we went to the women's unit.

As I recall, there were about four hundred women in there. Some of them were real beauties. There was one particularly good-looking woman who kept near Leon as he played. He didn't miss her attention.

When we finished the concert, Leon walked over and began talking to the good-looking woman. He said, "You let me know when you get out and how I can get in touch with you."

She smiled, then said, "It may be a while. But I certainly will let you know."

"Well, how long will it be?" asked Leon.

"I really don't know," she said.

"It can't be that long. What are you in for anyway?" he asked.

"I murdered my husband. I'm here for life," she said.

Leon was speechless. It was one of the few times I ever saw him that way.

There was an interesting thing that happened at the prison while the inmates were playing. They had a young man about twenty who played the trombone. He was out of this world. Not only could he play, but he was good-looking and had a great personality. Bob was attracted to him.

He was looking for a trombone player at the time. So

105

he got with the warden and found out that this young man was due to get out in a few months. The warden agreed to let him go early if Bob would agree to take his custody. Bob readily agreed to that. Within a few days, Bob had his trombone player.

He fit right in. He was a real good sport. The people liked him and he was simply great on the trombone. Since he had heard us so much, he already knew all our songs. But one of Bob's bitterest disappointments was about to happen.

It seemed that not all of the people liked the new trombone player. As much as the Oklahoma people loved Bob Wills, there was some self-righteousness there.

As soon as it got out that Bob had a jailbird in his band, we began to get nasty letters. People began saying they would not come to his dances if he didn't get rid of the convict. Bob was furious. He said, "I really don't give a damn what those self-righteous bastards think. There but for the grace of God and a lot of good luck, would be a lot of us."

So he bowed his head. He kept the trombone player.

But it didn't do any good. The criticism got worse and Bob finally had to face the reality that society was based on conventionalities. These people were going by the book. Bob let the young man go.

"That was the hardest thing I've ever done," he told me later. "It was like someone had my heart in a vice and they just kept on twisting it and I couldn't get a wedge in there to stop it."

He gave the guy $200 and told him if he ever needed any help to let him know. He had tears in his eyes the day the young man left.

I kept up with the young man. About a month later, he broke into a store and took some clothes. He was sent back to prison. I've got a theory on that. I think the kid did that because he didn't want Bob to have the responsibility of taking him back. He broke into that store to get Bob off the hook. But I will always have a fondness and a sadness in my heart for that young trombone player.

The trombone player, the little girl, the shut-ins and the sick are all good examples of how far Bob would go to help people. He did it for his band, too. There was no limit to how far he would go.

Sometimes these involved touchy issues. Like the time one of the boys who was married, came to Bob. He was downcast. He said, "Bob, I've been fooling around. I got a girl pregnant."

He told Bob all about it. It had started at the dances at the Trianon Ball Room. The girl had put the heavy rush on him. But he was true to his wife. But, she was good looking and she kept on after him, like an old hound dog that has struck a fox's path on a rocky trail, and there's just enough scent there to start him baying, and he knows sooner or later he's going to pick up the full trail. That's what this girl knew.

She was successful. She convinced the young man that the sky had no stars in it unless he was her star. If he would just love her fully one time, she could endure her drab life and would never bother him again. So he went to her room one night. The hound was baying on full trail.

About two months later, he went back to see her. He hadn't seen her in all that time. When he walked up, she said, "I've got news for you. I'm pregnant. I'm carrying your child." She broke into tears, then said, "I'll do anything to protect you. I'll kill myself."

The band member was shook! But he wasn't that shook. He had rather have a deceived wife than a dead woman on his hands. While he was struggling with his emotions, the girl said, "There is a solution. I know a doctor who can fix me for $150."

That was high money in those days. Musicians didn't make that kind of money and have it lying around. That's why the young man was so desperate. That's why he went to Bob.

Bob listened. His eyes were directly on the young man's face. When he got through his story, Bob said, "This may hurt, but I'm going to tell you something about your new true love. She is nothing but a fraud. She's a cheat. She's a tramp! Now here's what you do. You call her and you be real nice and sound concerned about her. But you tell her that you have a friend, a longtime high school buddy who went to medical school and is now a doctor and he will take care of her for you. Tell her that you will come and get her, bring her to Tulsa, put her in a room, and see that she gets expert care. Tell her you want to be near her and you want to be sure she is all right and you will pay for everything."

The young man called her and told her exactly what Bob had told him to. Guess what. He never heard from the girl again. About six months later, Bob asked him, "What ever happened to your lady friend?"

"I never heard from her since I called her," said the band member.

Bob shook his head and walked away grinning.

Bob helped me out many times. One of them was a very sad time in my life. It came when my wife died. She had gotten ill not too long after we moved to Tulsa. Eventually it was diagnosed as cancer. It was incurable.

The last few months were rough ones. She was in pain. No medicine helped her much. But I kept looking for something. Rather the doctors kept looking and I kept paying. By the time she died, all my savings were gone. I had also spent a bunch of borrowed money.

I went to Bob before the funeral. I told him my troubles. I said, "Bob, I need to borrow some money."

"How much do you need, kid?" he asked.

"I need $600," I said.

He didn't say anything else. He turned to Mayo and

108

told him to write me out a check. I had the money in a matter of minutes.

I took my wife's body back to Texas for burial. I also took a week off. I wanted to take more, but I kept thinking about how pressed I was for money. A friend had told me that I'd probably be better off back with the band where I wouldn't be spending so much time moping.

I kept my nose to the grindstone. I finally started getting things in order. My finances were shaping up. So after about five months, I asked Bob if I could talk to him. He, like always, said sure.

"Bob, I'm getting my finances back in shape and things are rolling pretty smoothly. I think I can start paying you that $600 back," I said.

"Kid, what are you talking about?" he asked.

"The money I got from you after my wife died. That $600," I said.

"I didn't loan you $600," said Bob.

"Yes you did, Bob. You had Mr. Mayo write out the check. You loaned it to me," I said.

"I *gave* you $600, kid. I didn't loan you nothing. And, I don't want to hear any more about it. You've got a lot of necessary things to worry about. Okay?" he said.

I stumbled out of his office that day. I couldn't talk. I walked out and the air smelled so good. There was a little wind kicking up. It felt cool on my face. It was drying my tears. That old Oklahoma sunshine looked like someone had sprinkled gold in front of me. Bob Wills had made it that way.

Chapter 11

THE 1930S, THOSE brutal but dazzling years — when people would save their pennies in a fruit jar so they could buy coffee and sugar, yet they would go out and blow a whole fifty cents to see a carnival.

When a firm that produced a product called Ovaltine took out huge ads in newspapers to proclaim its benefits. Those ads told about people drinking Ovaltine as a nightcap and falling asleep immediately and waking up in the morning filled with new strength and energy as a result of natural, refreshing sleep.

When people were turning out by the thousands to hear Bob Wills and His Texas Playboys. And we did our damndest to entertain them. We had plenty of chances. Because we went to plenty of places. One was near our home base. That was Oklahoma City. What a place!

We played in the Trianon Ball Room, which was in the downtown section. It was a nice roomy dance hall, located upstairs. It had a large bandstand. But, best of all, it had a really fine grand piano. Going there and playing that instrument was like thrusting my hands into a whirlpool bath. It really felt good, particularly after some of the dogs I'd played on.

110

We had us a favorite eating place in Oklahoma City. It was Beverly's Restaurant, about four blocks from the dance hall. We'd park our bus in front of Beverly's after each dance. We always left at 2 A.M. That was the orders from Bob. The driver left at two even if he was the only one there.

As in most places, there were lots of friendly women in Oklahoma City. Many of them came to see us. One night, one of the boys got hooked up with one of those friendly women. He wasn't ready when it was time for the bus to leave. The driver said, "Well, I'm leaving. That's orders."

We all hollered and laughed and got to singing:

"That's orders. That's orders. That's orders . . . from headquarters."

Naturally the band member had no way to get home. He knew he had to be back in Tulsa for our noon show. I guess he panicked. He found a way home. He called a cab and told the driver, "Take me back to Tulsa."

The driver did. When he let the guy out, he said, "Mister, this was one helluva fare. I bet I won't make this much working six days a week all of next month."

He probably wouldn't. Because it had been one helluva fare. It cost the band member two weeks' wages to pay it. He was never late again.

Sometimes when we were going to some place like Wichita Falls we'd get us a hotel room in Oklahoma City. Boys will be boys. So naturally, there was some feminine company involved. On one such occasion, the same woman entertained several of the boys.

That next Tuesday we were back playing at the Trianon. We had a new recruit with us on that trip. He was young and inexperienced about the ways of the world.

He met this woman and immediately thought he was in love. She really put the moves on him, like an experienced quarter horse does when it's cutting cattle out from the herd. That horse knows just which way to cut his feet and at which moment.

111

This young recruit brought his newly found love over to Beverly's after the dance. We all were there, already, eating our supper. The youngster had a grin a mile wide on his face. He said, "Boys, this is (her name). She's a lady."

Everyone just sat there. We felt like somebody had thrown catsup onto our white shirts. Finally, the guy got me off to the side and said, "Al, I think I'm in love. She says she feels the same way."

We all were dumbfounded. The fellow's new true love was the same woman who had entertained all of those boys just seven nights earlier. Somebody finally got him off to the side and explained the situation. He wouldn't believe him at first. Finally, the experienced band member said, "Well, tell me. Has she got a mole about two fingers above her navel?"

The young recruit got this funny look on his face. He looked like somebody had dumped catsup on him. He was heartbroken. For about two weeks.

We had this other modest and timid band member who was really girl shy. One night in Oklahoma City some of the boys sicced a seasoned woman on him. It would have taken an iron man to resist her advances. He wasn't an iron man.

One of the boys who had brought his car to the dance said he would take the timid boy and forward girl to her apartment. The boy agreed quickly. He literally ran out of the car to the woman's apartment.

In about thirty minutes he exploded from the front door, his shoes in his hand. He was shouting, "Get this car rolling. Hurry up, dammit. Her husband has come home unexpectedly."

We never really knew whether her husband had actually come home or not. But this man never went out with another girl all the time he was with the band.

Another place we went to occasionally was Medicine Park. It was a mountain resort near Lawton, Oklahoma. There was a big military base near Lawton. It was Fort

112

Sill. Things were very busy here during the prewar years and we played a dance at Medicine Park three or four times a year.

We played in a rather small ballroom in a hotel. It was hot in the summer and cold in the winter. The hospitality was the only comfortable thing about Medicine Park.

One of our guys had an interesting experience there. It was with one of the ugliest women I ever saw. She looked like wilted paint. She was masculine looking and had fuzzy red-dyed hair. She was also fat.

This member of the band had a pretty bad drinking problem. After every dance he would really hit the bottle. One night, about an hour after the dance at Medicine Park, we saw this old woman leading this guy off. You could tell by his eyes that he thought he had latched onto a queen. He later told us about what happened.

"Man, I thought I had the prettiest woman around. She was so cozy and warm and loving. I remember calling her my beautiful little peacock. Then I went to sleep.

"When I woke up, I felt something rubbing my face like sandpaper. I looked over and there was this bucket of ugly lying there beside me. I felt like I had woke up in a hog waller. She had a beard that needed shaving badly. She cuddled up close to me.

"Where in the name of God did you come from?" I asked her.

"She said, 'Honey, I'm your beautiful peacock. Remember?'

"Peacock, hell, get out of here before I call the manager."

He swore off of drinking after that. He stayed away from the liquor for at least a half a day. But that was a record for him.

I set a record of sorts for myself one time at Joplin. We played there many times and loved it. It was rough for me at first because there was a guy there who really loved Tommy on the piano. His name was Barney.

Everytime we played, Barney would stand up and start yelling about my playing.

"Bob, get Tommy back on the piano. This hayseed can't even play 'Jingle Bells,'" he would yell.

That happened every time we were in Joplin. For three years it happened. I felt like ringing this guy's bell. But, I never did. Finally, one night I was playing and it hit me all of a sudden. This guy wasn't hollering. He was actually listening to me play. After the dance he came over and put his arm around me.

"I gotta admit, Stricklin, you are a pretty good piano player," he said.

"Coming from you, Barney, that is the best compliment I have ever heard," I replied.

That wasn't the record I was talking about. The record happened one time when we got to Joplin early in the afternoon. We had several hours to kill before playing that night. Eldon Shamblin and I were standing out in front when some folks recognized us and invited us to come to their house and listen to some Bob Wills records. We went.

They had mixed up a big batch of whiskey sours. They invited us to have some. We debated the matter. Neither Eldon nor I were drinkers. And Bob had just recently repeated his law about no drinking before a performance.

But these people were so nice, and it was kinda hot, and those whiskey sours looked cool and inviting. Finally, I said, "Why not let's have just one, Eldon?"

"Why not?" he said.

So we did. But, that one was delicious. Then there was another one. Then another and another and finally it was time to go to the dance, and Eldon and I, the nondrinkers, were feeling no pain.

We tried to act like we were okay. But acting just made it worse. If you have ever tried to keep from laughing out loud in church when you were a kid, you know what we were going through. Bob was not mad. He was amused. The

114

curtain went up and Bob had the time of his life. So did Eldon and I.

He featured me on the piano that night more than ever before. My smile was so silly, my movements so ridiculous, that before long, the whole audience knew what was going on. Eldon and I nearly tore the house down. Bob, always quick to ride a winner, had Eldon do some numbers that he only occasionally did.

He did "Three Little Fishes," which was crazy when done even by a sober man. For an encore, he had Eldon do "You Gotta See Your Mama Every Night." On this number, sometimes the band would play a double or even a triple ending on the going-out chorus. That made it end something like this, "You gotta see your mama every night, or you can't see her at all."

This was the end of the song. But if the band played the double ending Eldon would sing the last phrase as a turnaround, saying, "I hear you talking," then "Can't see your mama at all." Then if the band played another ending, it would throw Eldon back to repeating, "I heard you talking," and the same routine again.

That night, the band played about six or seven of those endings and kept throwing Eldon back into that turnaround. To keep from saying, "I heard you talking," so many times, he started making up crazy things. It got to be hilarious.

I was funny enough. But then came my stunt at the piano. The bench was near the edge of a drop about eighteen inches to a lower level. Smokey was throwing his cigarette butts onto the keyboard as usual. That night, instead of worrying about missing the keys, I just sat on my hands to defend myself.

When I did that, the piano bench picked that time to slip off the level I was on. I couldn't catch myself since I was sitting on my hands. I just went off with the bench. So here I was upstaging Bob and Tommy, who were working the front mike. Because I was in front of that mike sitting on my hands.

The crowd thought it was part of the act. They cut loose with wild applause. They started cheering. They loved it.

Eldon and I began to lose our buzz going home that night. We got to worrying about what Bob would say or do to us. He never said anything.

We had us a great horn band going. That had happened, as I mentioned, because of Bob's efforts and ambitions to stay competitive. And we were really playing some good music. We got an offer to play for a fraternity dance at the University of Oklahoma at Norman. Bob was cool to the idea at first.

"Those college boys will just make fun of us and I don't like that," he told Mayo one day.

"Bob, you can play anything that anybody wants," said Mayo.

"Naw, we are just not their kind of people and it would be foolish for us to try to play the kind of music they like," said Bob.

"You've got a great array of horn men and fine arrangements like Tommy Dorsey. You can play for any kind of college people," insisted Mayo.

Bob finally agreed to play. We went over early on the day of the dance and visited the fraternity. We were shown around the campus and introduced to the athletes, coaches and everyone. The fraternity fed us a great supper.

That night the gym where the dance was was packed. Bob left his fiddle in the case. The band began to play "Woodchopper's Ball," "In the Mood," and "One O'Clock Jump." We sounded like Glen Miller. Or Tommy Dorsey. There was one problem. Nobody was dancing.

There were two things that made Bob mad. One was a fight starting. The other was when nobody would dance. Believe me, not one couple was dancing. They were just sitting on the sidelines looking. Maybe glaring is a better word.

"I knew we shouldn't have booked this job. I just knew

116

it," Bob told Tommy. About then, one of the college kids came up and asked if he could have a word with Bob.

"Mr. Wills," he said in a timid voice, "would you mind playing a number on your fiddle? Our favorite number at the fraternity house is 'Ida Red.' "

Bob started grinning. He took out his fiddle and started resining his bow. He said, "I'll see if I can oblige you, kid."

He sawed down on old "Ida Red." That dance floor filled up as quickly as a water glass does that is getting liquid pumped into it from a fire hose. The kids began to holler and shout and they were dancing so much I'd almost swear that you could see smoke coming out from their shoes. I think Bob began to realize after that dance that he had broken through to about everybody in that part of the country.

We'd go anywhere to play. If we had fans some place and they wanted to book us, we'd go. That's the reason many people probably never heard of some of the places we played at. One of those places was Hominy, Oklahoma, about fifty miles from Tulsa. It was perched in the middle of a big Indian reservation.

We played there about every three months. We played at the armory. The people were great. The enthusiasm was great. There was one bad thing, though. They had the sorriest piano I ever played on. Tommy had attacked it. The few notes and hammers that were left were damaged. The strings that were not broken were so out of tune that you really couldn't play the thing at all.

We played there off and on for seven years. That piano was never repaired or tuned or fixed. I used to think about going there. I hated that piano so much that I would dream about it. Then I would get sick sometimes on the day we were supposed to go. Bob didn't really blame me. He knew the situation.

But one day, after about three years, a friend and big booster of the band was having a showing of the new model

117

Chevrolets at his dealership. He wanted Bob to come and play the noon broadcast from his place.

Bob accepted. He told me, "Al, when we go to Hominy this time, we are going to a place that is bound to have a good piano. You'll enjoy it. I promise you."

It sounded good. The boys even rejoiced with me. On the way to Hominy that morning, they started making up little songs about the new piano. The guy's name that had hired us was Cal Newport. The song went:

> Cal is good to Al.
> He had his pal, a new piano you see.
> And, if he plays,
> He always stays,
> With the other boys in the same key.

I thought it was cute. I was feeling good. I was looking forward to playing that new piano. We arrived and I was one of the first off of the bus. I nearly ran inside the place. The first thing I saw was the piano. I wanted to throw up. Would you believe they had moved that old sorry-ass piano in there from the armory.

Something happened at the armory that I'll never forget. One night I was going in and they had this high school girl working the door. She wouldn't let me in unless I paid the ticket.

"But, I'm Al Stricklin," I told her.

"I never heard of you. Pay me please," she said.

Finally, the man who ran the show came along and told the girl to let me in. I found out later the girl had never worked the dance. She didn't even like our music.

I still get a lot of laughs about that. Maybe I should say we get a lot of laughs. That girl was Betty Zeigler. Today, she is Mrs. Al Stricklin.

When you are playing before so many thousands of people, and they're paying out their money to hear you, you've just got to expect to take some crap from the crowd.

118

Most of the people we played to were gracious and friendly and wouldn't think about getting out of hand. But you put that many people together and you're going to get some bad ones sometimes. They're going to start sweating and they're going to start smelling a little bad and their heads are going to get fuzzy, and sometimes there is just no way you can avoid trouble.

But Bob was a master at handling the crowds. He could take just about anything from the people in the audience. He took an awful lot. He told me one time, "Kid, those people kinda own the band. We are supposed to give them what they want."

We did. But, sometimes, a smart-alec would just keep on popping off and screaming and Bob would get a bellyful and he would set them down.

One time we were playing for a grand opening of a big furniture store in Tulsa. It was called "Pig Skin Davis." While we were playing a number, a teen-age girl started hollering. She moved close to the bandstand and screamed as loud as she could.

"Aah-haa," she shouted.

It was obvious she was making fun out of Bob and us. This time he stopped the band immediately. The crowd got quiet quickly. Bob pointed his finger right at the girl and said, "Some folks make a living acting like a damn fool and some don't."

Everybody remained quiet. The girl ducked her head and started walking out. The crowd came to its feet. They began applauding wildly.

There was another time that Bob pulled a master trick with a heckler. This happened one night when we were playing a dance. A man kept hollering at Bob that if he couldn't beat Bob Wills playing the fiddle he would turn in his badge.

"Hell, he ain't nothing but a hick. I'll bet he never even went to school," screamed the man.

Bob took it for thirty minutes. I noticed that spot on

119

BOB WILLS AND his Playboys at the National Guard Armory in Hominy, Oklahoma, 1938.

PLAYBOYS POSE for the photographer at the Blue Moon Open Air dance pavilion, Tulsa, 1939.

the back of his neck was getting red. I knew he was about to take some kind of action. I halfway expected that he might just smash the guy over the head with his fiddle. No, I really didn't expect that. But, deep down inside, I was wishing that he would.

Finally, right in the middle of a number, Bob stopped and dropped his fiddle. He looked at the heckler and said, "You, mister come up here. You folks there (he pointed at a table) just lead him right on up here."

The people didn't need much encouraging. They practically lifted the guy up on the bandstand. He looked embarrassed and kept trying to find a place to put his hands. His pockets weren't deep enough.

"Here's my fiddle, friend. Now, ladies and gentlemen, we want you to listen to a man who can play a fiddle better than me. We all know he can because he's been telling us this all night long. Okay, mister, show us how good you are."

The man turned red and then green. He choked up. He handed Bob back the fiddle. He mumbled, "Mr. Wills, I was wrong."

He went back and sat down. He never heckled us again.

Things were moving. You could buy a house for $150 down and twenty-two dollars a month and that included interest, principal and taxes and insurance. People were reading "Popeye" and "Bringing Up Father" and "Andy Gump." Mae West had been threatened with bodily damage by some nuts who were going to douse her with acid if she didn't pay them ransom.

U.S. Royal Company had come up with a tire called the "Royal Master." It had the grip of a "centipede" the ads said.

We were about to get that kind of grip on the public with some songs. One of them was going to be another recording of "The Old San Antonio Rose." It would be "The New San Antonio Rose." It would give all us sweet smells of success.

120

Chapter 12

A S I SAID, we made the original "Rose" in May, 1938. It sold pretty good. It was a typical Bob Wills tune. Easy to follow and understand and not bogged down with a lot of intricacies. It made you feel the wind blowing and you could see the farmers struggling against the wind and drought and feeling like they were whipped but all of the time they knew they weren't because somewhere out there floating on the clouds beyond the burning sun was hope. The melody put that hope into the hearts of people. I didn't feel like "Rose" portrayed that a lot more than some of Bob's other tunes, but it did have that little extra something.

In the ensuing two years Bob kept fiddling around with words for the tune. He and other members of the band were always putting lines together and then remodifying them and working them over again. Bob was that way. He wanted the words to be perfect.

He and Tommy worked hardest on it, I guess. They finally got the first verse. Then they went to work on the chorus. Then they proceeded to the next verse. So it went. Until on April 15, 1940, we were back in Dallas for another recording session. I always find that date kinda ironic now. That was the date we recorded "The New San Antonio Rose." As you all know, that is income tax deadline now. Believe me, Bob made a ton of money to pay income taxes on from that song.

In that recording session we had Jesse Ashlock on the fiddle, along with Bob; Tommy Duncan, singing; Leon McAuliffe, steel guitar; Louis Tierney, fiddle and sax; Eldon Shamblin, guitar; Johnnie Lee Wills, banjo; Son Lansford, bass; me, piano; Everett Stover, trumpet; Wayne Johnson, clarinet; Tiny Mott, sax; Smokey Dacus, drums; and Tubby Lewis, trumpet. Mr. Satherly and Mr. Law were the producers.

The songs we recorded that session were, "You Don't Love Me," "No Wonder," "Lone Star Rag," "There's Going to Be a Party," "I Don't Love Nobody," "That Brownskin Gal," "Corine Corinna," "Let Me Call You Sweetheart," "Blue Bonnet Rag," "Time Changes Everything," "Medley of Spanish Waltzes," "Bob Wills Special," "Big Beaver," and "The New San Antonio Rose."

Some of those songs broke the dam. Some were property of other people, but most of them were Bob's very own. He had thought them up, worked on them and prepared them for the recording session.

There's no doubt that the old "Rose" was a hit. But it was not the instant hit the new "Rose" was. The words, with the music, were a winning combination. Once on the market, they spread like a huge net across the nation, catching the hearts of the people. And not only here but in many parts of the world.

We knew it was a hit when Bob came in one day with a handful of letters and telegrams. All told him how great "Rose" was. He got hundreds of congratulatory messages. Record sales boomed. Soon it was at the top or near the top in sales of all times.

Bing Crosby recorded "San Antonio Rose." He sent Bob a personal telegram telling him how great he thought the song was. A movie company made a movie called

122

"San Antonio Rose." It bought the movie rights to the title.

The dignitaries of Tulsa, led by the mayor, had a big night in Bob's honor. They had it at a very exclusive club. We played. In the middle of the ceremonies the mayor stood up and said, "Friends, some people in this country call him a country bumpkin. Some people kid him about his country flavor. But, we the people in Tulsa don't. Neither does Bing Crosby. He has sent us a telegram telling us how fortunate we are to have such a great musician living in our city. We are proud of that. We are proud of *Bob Wills*."

The crowd stood on its feet. Thunderous applause rang out. It kept on going and going like a fire that can't be stopped. Bob had the city of Tulsa eating out of his hand and he had people on their feet applauding him who, a few years ago, were turning their noses up at us like they do when they walk by an outdoor toilet. That was a great night.

"San Antonio Rose" attracted another person's attention. That was Irving Berlin. He sent one of his scouts down to spend a couple of weeks with us. Berlin was going to publish "San Antonio Rose."

The scout was a friendly little guy. He weighed about 125 pounds. This was his first trip to the south. It took him a few days to make adjustments. Tommy cut several of his ties off. Then one day while we were rehearsing he came in late, looking kind of bleary-eyed. He sat down, and all of a sudden several of us ran over to him and began tearing his shirt off. We didn't complete the job. But we left the shirt in shreds. He said, "By Jesus God, you fellows are really getting out of hand sometimes." But he became a good sport. In a few days he was a first-class-Playboy and traveling companion.

When he left, you could tell he hated to go. He got choked up. He said, "I've really enjoyed this, men. The people love you. You draw good crowds. They love you.

I really hate to go. It's been two of the best weeks of my life. And, I'll never forget you. Because I love you."

He gave Berlin a fine report. Somebody later told us it was the finest report he had ever given. It must have been. Because The Berlin Company soon put "San Antonio Rose" on sheet music and orchestrations.

"Rose" brought us many memorable experiences. But the best single episode happened while we were playing a dance at San Antonio, Texas, a few months after the song hit the top. The job had been booked down there several weeks ahead. That gave the city plenty of time to prepare for our coming.

We made the trip while on a two-weeks' tour. We had played San Angelo and headed out for San Antonio. It was about a four-hour trip. We turned on our radio in the bus and listened to a San Antonio station.

It seemed every commercial was about our coming. The disc jockey would say, "And, they're going to be here tonight. He, and his band. Bob Wills and His Texas Play-boys — the man and the men who have put our town on the lips of recognition even in England."

One disc jockey went even further. He said, "Only one other person has given San Antonio this kind of publicity and notoriety. That man was David Crockett, the hero of the Alamo."

Bob was with us in the bus this trip. Generally, he drove his own car. But he had wanted to ride with us on our triumphant trip to the city. He kept smiling as he listened to the radio. He said, "Boys, you'd never have thought an old country boy from Turkey, who once cut hair, would ever be up this high spinning around in success."

Everyone knew what hotel we were going to stay in. So there was quite a mob at the place. The city had sent over three dozen policemen to handle the crowd. We were glad they did. It took us about an hour to work our way into the lobby.

124

People were hollering and screaming and stomping their feet. They were thrusting pens and movie cameras into our faces and begging for autographs. They had gone wild.

Bob was having a tough battle. The news media were interviewing him about everything. One said, "Mr. Wills, what do you think of the German invasion of Europe?" He was a celebrity.

He finally made it to his room. It was not much better there. They had to get him another room.

The rest of us were having our problems also. I decided to go and stay with some relatives in order to get some rest. I put on some old khakis and a work shirt in order to slip out. Somebody spotted me as I was walking down the stairs. He yelled, "Hey, aren't you a Texas Playboy?"

A crowd of people looked up. I could almost hear their thundering hoofbeats coming toward me. I ducked my head and shook it and kept on walking. Thank gosh, I made it to my relatives.

They had the radio on. Reporters were interviewing Bob about everything. They were quoting him on everything he said. One of my relatives said, "Alton, you had better prepare yourself for a wild time tonight. The people are going to give you a welcome you'll never forget."

How right he was.

The dance had been scheduled for the Civic Auditorium, a big barrellike place with lots of seats and space. They were going to need it. Tickets had been sold out weeks in advance. Some people were standing outside of the auditorium.

"I've got one hundred dollars. One hundred in cash, for one, just one ticket to the Bob Wills Dance," one man in a nice suit and straw hat was saying. He got no takers.

We left the hotel by the back entrance. We were trying to be secret. We left about one-and-a-half hours ahead of time. We wanted to get there before the jam started. We weren't successful. There were already thousands of people on the streets and around the hotel.

It took us thirty minutes to work our way from the hotel to the auditorium. That's only a block and a half away. Again, they had called out dozens of police to help control the crowd.

"I just want to touch one of them," shouted a woman, her voice raw and deep like the sound of a big ripsaw cutting through a thick piece of timber.

We finally reached the auditorium and got inside. It was already packed. It looked like someone had jammed 10,000 matches into a penny matchbox.

We set up our instruments and then ran for the dressing room. We were looking for some place to hide. We were really afraid for our own safety. We stayed there until just before 9 P.M. Finally, we went out and started playing. Thank God our theme song was not "San Antonio Rose."

But, as if by signal, these 2,000 voices began shouting. They were drowning out our music. But we could hear what they were saying.

" 'San Antonio Rose.' 'San Antonio Rose.' Come on Bob," they were screaming.

It was like the star halfback of a football team was leading his team to victory. The fans wanted a touchdown. These fans wanted their city's song.

Bob waited for about an hour. We kept right on playing for dancing. But nobody was dancing. They couldn't, in that mass of humanity. Besides, nobody wanted to.

Finally, about 10 P.M., Bob said, "Okay, fellows, let's play it now. And we will probably be doing our next talking when we get back to the hotel."

I know the audience sensed what was going to be played. They tensed up all of a sudden. There was just a short pause, like there is between lightning and thunder. Then, we began playing it — "The New San Antonio Rose."

I'd never heard bedlam like that before. It was like having 10,000 giant beds inside a hall and all of a sudden all of the bed slats fall out and there's a rising clap of noise.

After our first few notes, none of us or none of them

126

heard anything. We were just going through the motions as far as the crowd was concerned. The noise was deafening. Eldon was nearest me and I could not hear a note he was playing. We were together when it was over. That was from habit, I guess.

After the crowd settled down, we played for another hour and then we played "Rose" again. This time the crowd listened to it pretty good. I remember hearing one woman tell her date or husband, "By damn, honey, it does sound pretty after all."

That's got to be one of the greatest nights of my career with Bob Wills. We were on top. We were the honey for the buttered biscuits. We were famous. People knew us by our first names. People we'd never heard of. It was a great feeling. It was a supreme night.

And, for awhile, we forgot about the ominous headlines in the newspapers and the news we'd been hearing on the radio about Hitler and his troops goose-stepping their way across Europe, conquering country after country. I guess, even that night, those of us who were realists and really thought about it knew that it was going to end. Because our country was going to war, it seemed like. War meant armies. Armies meant men. The Texas Playboys would respond. But there would be some more good times before it all happened.

Chapter 13

TODAY, IT'S HARD to imagine that anyone would use a horse to get them to places. You see all of the cars roaring down the freeways, and you hear the ads on the radio and television talking about how many horsepower a certain car's engine has, and it's some intangible sort of thing that you hear and think more in terms of some long row of powerful pistons connected to some giant spark plugs that are constantly being hit with little flashes of electricity and thundering sounds come pouring out a muffler. You don't think of horses, as such.

But back in the 1930s there still were plenty of people who used horses. And Bob loved horses. He had some fine ones. He insisted that the band become interested in horses, too. Because as many rodeos and fairs as we played at, Bob had made horses a part of our act.

At this time Bob had a ranch northwest of Tulsa. The Old Chisholm Trail, which had been used for so many cattle drives to the Kansas City market in the 1800s, cut through Bob's ranch.

Bob decided that all of us should own a horse. He said he would keep the horses at his ranch. He said everyone should ride a horse. That meant a new learning process.

Because a lot of the band had never ridden a horse. But, we started learning.

It was a painful experience. Particularly for our rear ends. We'd go out there on the ranch, saddle up, and bob up and down for hours, our ends really taking a beating. One day one of the band members said, after a particularly arduous and trying day in the saddle, "If God had meant for man to ride horses, He would have built man a pillow in his ass."

We kept at it. When we finally got to where Bob thought we were good enough, we rode our horses in parades and at grand entries in the rodeos.

We trained and trained one particular feat. That was to enter the arena, go at a dead run to the center, rein our horse in, raise our hat and wave to the crowd as the horse rared up. The crowd loved it. It sounds easy. But it took many hours to learn the technique. Many asses were busted as we learned. One man said, "If God had intended man to ride into an arena and do this, He would have built nests of feathers in the ground for him to land upon."

We had a very fine trumpet player named Tubby Lewis join our band. He could play that trumpet like a genius. He couldn't ride worth a damn. He never learned how. One thing in his way was his weight. Tubby weighed about 350 pounds.

Tubby was fearful from the first. He just didn't think he had the strength to pull himself onto a horse. We solved that by getting a ladder. There was another problem. They had to find a giant horse that was strong enough to carry him. They finally found one. His name was Old Les.

The first time Tubby mounted Old Les, we had the ladder. Tubby eased his way up the ladder and finally threw his right leg over and plumped down into the saddle. It sounded like someone had taken a big spoonful of mashed potatoes and dropped them from about the height of a foot onto a plate. Les, a gentle horse, tolerated it quite

129

well. He looked back at Tubby as if to say, "Now I've seen everything."

Tubby never became an accomplished rider. But he was a sport. So what we did to get him introduced turned out to be one of the funniest things I've ever seen.

The announcer would say, "Now ladies and gentlemen, we have Tubby Lewis racing out on Old Les."

Tubby, while all of this was going on, would be behind the arena getting his nerve up to get on the horse. He really had to psych himself. He'd say, "Okay, I'll do it just this one more time, Lord, if You'll just keep me from falling and I promise You I won't eat another whole apple pie at one setting again until next month."

We would then lead Les out in the entrance of the arena. We would put the ladder in place. Tubby would come out, climb the ladder and plop down into the saddle. Then one of us would lead the horse to the center of the arena and the announcer would say, "Take your bow, Tubby."

Tubby would raise his hat, all the time gripping the horn of the saddle like it was the only thing keeping him from going down into a bed of quicksand. We would lead him to the other side of the arena, put the ladder back up and he would crawl down. The crowd always loved it.

One rodeo that I'll never forget was the one at Dewey, Oklahoma. We played music there for several years. One time we were just getting ready to start and the announcer said, "Ladies and gentlemen, we have the honor today of having in our audience 300 Royal Air Force cadets. They are stationed nearby and are training to be fighter pilots to aid their beloved England in her struggle against Nazi Germany. These fine young men have never seen or heard the great Bob Wills and His Texas Playboys. So I feel it would be a nice gesture on our part if we showed our friendship for their country and our appreciation of them if instead of the usual national anthem, we would have Mr. Wills and his band play the English national anthem, 'God

130

Save the King.' Now, we bring you the great Texas Playboys and 'God Save the King.' "

There was one problem. None of us had any idea of what "God Save the King" sounded like. In times like this, Bob always turned to Everett Stover for him to start the song. But Everett didn't know the song. He whispered to Bob, "Goddammit, I don't know it."

Bob turned to me. He whispered, "Al, you are a school-teacher, don't you know, 'God Save the King'?"

"I wish to hell I did, but I don't," I whispered. I was sitting on my hands again. I wasn't tight this time.

"Don't any of you know the thing?" Bob pleaded with the rest of the band.

All he got was silence.

Then the announcer said, "Mr. Wills, we are waiting."

It looked like the end of the world for us. Can you imagine our embarrassment. Here were these fine young Englishmen over here training for the defense of their country and we didn't even know their national anthem. Damn, it looked bad.

Then all of a sudden a little girl with pigtails stuck her head out from behind the piano. She looked to be about ten. She whispered to me, "Mister, if you-all can play 'America,' you'll have it made."

"Are you certain, sweetheart?" I asked her.

"I'm certain because just the other day our teacher taught us the words and the tune," she said.

"You're going to heaven, honey, if you never do nothing else good," I said, as I began to strike the chord on the piano.

I told Everett to sock it to "America." He did. The rest of us joined in. Who said we couldn't play "God Save the King"? If a ten-year-old girl could save the Texas Playboys, we could save the king. We played the hell out of that song.

After we finished, these young Englishmen snapped to attention. They let out a great cheer. The rest of the crowd joined in. When the rodeo was over, many of the cadets came over and shook our hands and got our autographs. One of them said, "We want our families and friends to see what the greatest band in America looks like."

They don't know how close that greatest band came to being the most embarrassed band.

In those days, people were still paying homage to the great Will Rogers who was killed in August, 1935. Many times when we were playing a rodeo, they would lead a riderless horse to the center of the arena. We would play "Empty Saddles." Then we would play Rogers' most favorite song, "Old Faithful." People wept openly when this happened.

Those rodeos were what is called a happening today. There were banners all over the streets and downtown stores. There generally would be a lot of big-shot politicians when the event opened. We'd always ride in those parades. Bob usually rode up front with the dignitaries.

One time the governor was riding up front. People started waving and shouting. Not at the governor, but at Bob Wills. He had on his well-tailored western suit and was riding Punkin, that great stallion, saddled with that beautiful silver-lined saddle that George the Hamburger King had given him. It was a beautiful sight. It hurt the governor's feelings. He didn't like a band leader getting more applause than him.

We went out to Bob's ranch about twice each week to practice our riding. It was only about a ten-minute drive from Cain's Academy. But one day, when we were not supposed to practice riding, Bob told Tommy to tell us that there was going to be some excitement at the ranch. Punkin, then about three years old, was going to breed a mare for the first time.

Punkin had a long line of papers. He had fine bloodlines. Bob knew he was going to make some money off of him in stud fees. He wanted us to see that first time. So we all went.

There were about eight of us to witness the great event. We were all lined up on the tall board fence waiting for the action. Punkin, who was truly a beautiful stallion with rippling muscles, was led out. The boys got real quiet like they had been at that house in Chicago. They could tell that Punkin was going to perform.

He did his job expertly. He seemed to enjoy it. When he was finished, both his body and the body of the mare were wet, with little white streaks popping up from their slick, muscled quarters. That's when I heard a great commotion. Several of the band members had jumped from the fence and ran to their cars. They were leaving clouds of dust as they roared away toward home and their wives.

One of them hung his foot in the fence. He jerked it loose so quickly, he tore the board loose. He was running to his car. The reason I know he was running is because I was right behind him. We were going home to Mama.

That night we showed up for the job. Bob was already there. He came by grinning. He said, "Say, why did you boys rip splinters into your ass getting off of that fence in such a hurry? Did you get hungry or something?"

He pulled off his hat and slapped it on his thigh. He broke up laughing. He said, "I wonder if I could bottle old Punkin's magic up and sell it as an aphrodisiac?"

He started laughing again.

One of the best practical jokes I ever saw pulled on Bob happened at a dance after one of the big rodeos. Jesse did it. Jesse was the damndest wart you ever saw. You just could never tell when he was kidding or serious. Bob, being serious about entertaining people, was a plum for Jesse to pull these jokes on.

On this particular night Bob and Jesse were playing two fiddles on a beautiful waltz at a big dance. Bob, as was customary, would play a verse and Jesse would step back until time to come in with the harmony. This time as Jesse stepped up to play with Bob, he whispered to Bob,

133

MRS. BOB (Betty) WILLS

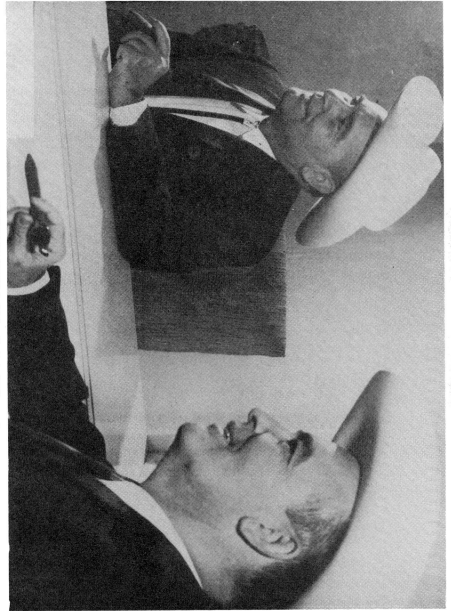

WESTERN SWING "King", Bob Wills, 1960.

"Bob, for God's sake, your pants are unbuttoned and standing wide open."

Bob was never knock-kneed before in his life. But at that moment he developed the damndest case of instant knock-kneedness you'd ever seen. He was close to crossing his legs. I know he was dying to turn around and button his pants. But he didn't. He kept playing. He had the silliest look on his face. He was in a half crouch, half cross-legged, knock-kneed stance and the embarrassed look on his face was almost too much.

He finally finished the song. He said later it seemed like it took him all night to do it. He ran for the back. He put his fiddle down and bent down to button his pants. That's when he found out his pants were not unbuttoned. The embarrassed look changed to one of fury. Immediately. He said, "Jesse, you little sonofabitch, I'm going to kill you for this."

The whole band got tickled. We were breaking up. Bob got over his anger as quickly as it had started when he realized how funny it was and how tickled everyone else was. Then he got tickled. Somehow the audience caught on. They started laughing.

Bob said later it was the most embarrassing, furious moment of his life.

We were having such good successes at the rodeos that Bob decided he would produce a rodeo. That was in 1938. He rented a big arena in Tulsa. He called it the "Bob Wills Stampede." It was going to run Thursday through Sunday.

Many of his friends and co-workers tried to discourage Bob. They said it would cost too much, having to bring in so many horses, bulls, steers and all of the other necessary ingredients for a rodeo. But Bob went ahead with his plans.

The day of the first show something happened that made us all jumpy. A picture and a story of Bob ran in the *Tulsa World*. It was on the front page. It was about Bob's taking his fourth wife. Everyone thought the attendance would fall because of this gossip. Bob just laughed.

134

"Hell, don't you guys know people better than that? There will be thousands here just to see if I have any horns," he said.

He was right. All four shows were sellouts. Bob made a killing off of the event. So much so that it turned out to be an annual event.

One time during the show we had a near calamity. It was on a Sunday afternoon. It happened just after the final bull had been ridden. The big, snorting bull was being herded toward the entrance when suddenly he let out with a big beller and jumped.

He cleared a board wall about seven feet high. He bellered again and ran right up a stairway aisle. When he got to the top, he started circling the area that went all the way around the top part of the arena.

The announcer cautioned everyone to remain in their seats. The bull made about three rounds without trying to head into the crowd of people. Finally, one cowboy and then another got up there and started roping the bull. They got about six ropes around him, pulled him down, tied his legs and bumped him down the stairs and back to the arena.

Many women were screaming. Many men were screaming. Some fainted. Some had to be taken to the hospital. Bob reacted with his usual quickness. He told Mayo to go to every person's room who had been taken to the hospital from the rodeo and tell them that Bob Wills was paying all expenses of the ambulance and hospital. He then asked them to sign releases.

You know, we never heard a word of complaint about that incident. Not even the murmur of a suit. I'm sure it was not only because of Bob's quick thinking, but because he really gave a damn about those people's welfare and they knew it.

Bob thought a lot about the band's welfare. Like one day when I was out at the ranch practicing my riding. I got off and went over to get a drink of water. Bob saw me and

135

walked over. He watched the other guys and smiled and said, "Kid, I've got great plans for this ranch. Some long-range plans. We're going to start a colony here someday. It will be the retirement place for all of the Texas Playboys.

"We'll all build us houses out here and we'll live here with our families. It will be great. We can still play some and ride our horses and just watch each other grow old peacefully."

It was a royal idea. The other Playboys liked it. So did I. Many of us had already started little savings accounts in which we were stockpiling some money for the day when we'd come out there and build our homes.

But it never happened. Too many clouds of change were in the future. We eventually would be breaking up. But I don't think any of us have ever forgotten the idea, nor stopped wondering how it would have been living out there in the open just an "ah-ha" away from the rest of the Playboys.

Chapter 14

THE WAR WAS getting near. You could almost smell it. Certainly, you heard about it over radio and read about it in the newspapers. Many were carrying day-by-day summaries.

But you could still buy yourself a big six-cubic-foot Crosley refrigerator for $11.95. And you could buy yourself a pint of Glenmore Bourbon for $1.00 and a quart for $1.95. Radios were selling for $3.00 to $5.95 and the last one was guaranteed to get at least five stations. And we were still running into some funny things.

Like the time we were en route to Fayetteville, Arkansas and we stopped at this big package store and curio shop that was owned by Trigger and Jack Holt, both great friends and fans of ours. We always tried to stop and visit them. One time I went into the restroom.

On the wall in this very clean and nice room was a Sears catalogue, some toilet paper and three corncobs. I knew what a corncob was for because I had been reared on a farm. But the three corncobs needed an explanation. They had been considerate enough to write one and nail it underneath the cobs. It said:

"Use one red cob. Then a white cob to see if you need another red cob."

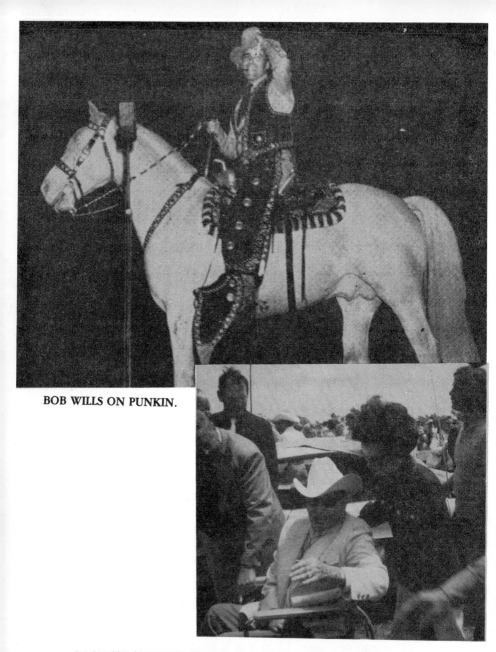

BOB WILLS ON PUNKIN.

BACK TO TURKEY, TEXAS—In 1973 Bob Wills returned to his boyhood home of Turkey, Texas for Bob Wills Day. He is shown here with his wife, Betty, Al Stricklin, Leon McAuliffe, and Bill Johnson, Bob's brother-in-law.

PROOF THAT EVERY member of Bob Wills' Texas Playboys had his own horse to ride. This photo was made near the Blue Moon Dancing Club in the summer of 1938. Left to right: Bob Wills on Punkin, Smokey Dacus, Eldon Shamblin, Tiny Mott, Johnnie Lee Wills, Zeb McNally, Herman Arnspiger, Joe Ferguson, Everett Stover, Son Lansford, Leon McAuliffe, Jesse Ashlock, Al Stricklin, Tubby Lewis, Tommy Duncan, and O. W. Mayo.

There was no doubt that the country was thinking about war. They called up the 45th Army Division. Prior to all of the activity, it was made up mostly of Oklahoma boys with some Texans. Lots of those guys had been going to Bob's dances all over Oklahoma since they were big enough to dance. Hundreds of them were just like our own kids.

Early in 1940 the 45th was called up and sent to Abilene, Texas, for a few months. There were national guardsmen from a wide area involved in this call-up. All went to the big army base at Abilene.

They had been there a few months and were getting lonesome. Some of the boys began to request that Bob Wills come out there and play a dance. So a promoter booked us there on a weekend night at a large building at the city's fairgrounds. It turned out to be a horrible mistake.

We began to see the mistake almost as soon as these young soldiers began coming into the dance hall. They had been cooped up for months. They were eager to get out and relax, have a few drinks and dance to the music of Bob Wills and His Texas Playboys. That was all right. But the trouble was, very few of them had dates when they arrived.

So you had hundreds of young soldiers who were stag. I think there were only about 200 people with escorts. That's not very many women to go around.

It didn't take long for things to start getting out of hand. The young soldiers, not having anyone to dance with, started crowding around the bandstand. They began to get rowdy.

They kept drinking. They got louder and bolder. They began to crawl up on the bandstand with us. Pretty soon, there was no doubt about what was happening. The soldiers were out of control. The few police there just could not begin to handle them.

"Hey, Mr. Policeman, if you'll pull off that gun, you'd

pass for a good dancing partner and I'd just love to dance with you," one of them yelled.

By 10:30 Bob knew what was going to happen. He told us he was going to slip out. He wasn't scared. He was just being realistic.

By 11:00 many of the young boys felt like they had to dance. They began to forcefully grab partners from the civilian men. The civilians didn't like that. So several fist-fights erupted.

The civilians began leaving. The young soldiers began grabbing men and started dancing with them. One of them hollered, "Hell, riding a mule is better than not riding at all."

By 11:30 it was turmoil. The manager came over and shouted to us, "If you can get out, you'd better. I think this is getting out of hand."

Just as he finished a folding chair sailed over his head. About then we began to feel like the manager was right. So we started sneaking out.

As we were loading our instruments carloads of MPs began arriving. When they went inside it sounded like a herd of cattle had been turned loose inside the auditorium. They started dragging the boys who had passed out or had been knocked out out of the building by the dozens. They were tossing them into trucks just like we used to toss bales of hay on the wagons back on the farm.

When we got back to the hotel it was full of soldiers and prostitutes. After we got to our room a call girl would knock every few minutes. It was pure bedlam.

The funny thing about it was that Abilene had the reputation of being one of the cleanest towns morally anywhere. It had several private church schools and there were more churches and church people living there than probably any town its size in Texas. But it was just a victim of the prewar craze that was snaking across the nation.

Things were moving fast in the nation. And they were moving fast for Bob. In 1940 he made his first movie. It was a full-length movie with an established star. That was Tex Ritter. The movie was *Take Me Back to Oklahoma*.

Bob could only take six of us out there that first time. But he assured us that there were going to be other movies, and eventually all of us would get our turn. It wasn't my turn on that first trip.

They had the world premier of *Take Me Back to Oklahoma* on August 9-11, 1940, at the Rialto Theatre in Tulsa. It turned out to be the largest wingding that the city had ever had.

We all appeared with Bob and Tex Ritter. The radio stations carried news items about the event. The newspapers were full of it. Crowds started fighting for tickets to the theatre three days ahead of time. One of the newspaper stories read:

> Bob Wills, the one-time cotton picker of Texas who rode to fame on his fiddle, will parade at 10 A.M. Saturday with Tex Ritter, a cowboy star of motion pictures, in a ballyhoo for *Take Me Back to Oklahoma,* which is showing Saturday, Sunday and Monday at the Rialto.
>
> Wills will ride his Palomino stallion while Ritter will ride a borrowed horse, James Ranch Silver Cloud, another stallion.
>
> Behind the two cowboys will ride a parade of six cars and the 15 men of the Wills orchestra on horseback.
>
> Lieut-Gov. James Berry will ride in the parade. Berry is an old-time friend of Wills.
>
> Route of the parade will be: Start at Fifth and Elgin, thence on Fifth to Boston, North on Boston to Second, thence West on Second to Main, thence South on Main to Seventh, thence East on Seventh to Frankfort.

Thence we were to play and everyone was to have a

helluva time. I guess they did. Thousands turned out. They danced in the aisles and shouted all through the movie.

In February, 1941, we made another bunch of records in Dallas. Our band then included: Bob and Louis Tierney, fiddles; Tommy Duncan, vocals; Leon McAuliffe, steel guitar; Eldon Shamblin, standard guitar; Son Lansford, bass; me, piano; Tubby Lewis and Jamie McIntosh, trumpets; Wayne Johnson, sax and clarinet; Don Harlan, sax and clarinet; Granville King, sax; Zeb McNally, sax; and Gene Tomlin, drums.

The records we made were released on O.K. Labels. They were "Lyla Lou," "My Worried Mind," "Maiden's Prayer," "Oh You Pretty Woman," "I Knew the Moment I Lost You," "Done and Gone," "Twin Guitar Special," "Takin' It Home," and "Take Me Back to Tulsa."

There's been quite a few stories told about "Take Me Back to Tulsa." Actually, the idea for the song started about 1936. We'd be away from home and tired and one of the boys would say, "I wanna go home. Take me back to Tulsa."

We got to saying it so much that one day one of the boys on the bus said, "Somebody ought to write a song about that. It'd make a helluva hit."

Bob, always alert and on the lookout for a new song, grabbed hold of the suggestion. He came up with a simple fiddle number. Actually, it was a breakdown. The tune had the kind of freedom that you could put dozens of verses to and Tommy and the boys obliged.

When Bob made the movie, *Take Me Back to Oklahoma*, it seemed to create a pressing need for him to go ahead and push the song with a similar title. That was the birth of "Take Me Back to Tulsa."

The song is unusual in that it has the same melody for the verses as it has for the chorus. It had these many verses, but the chorus was a repeat each time except the going-out chorus.

I would be the first to admit that I never thought this song would be a hit. I just didn't think it had a chance. It was too simple. But I should have learned my lesson from "San Antonio Rose." It became a great hit because it was a simple melody, easy to play and easy for the average person to learn.

"Take Me Back to Tulsa" turned out to be one of the top four songs that Bob ever did. First, of course, was "San Antonio Rose." Then came "Faded Love" and "Steel Guitar Rag," which was and is the property of Leon Mc-Auliffe.

In July, 1941, Bob was going to take me to Hollywood. We all went. We were going to make another movie and also do another bunch of recordings.

The person who wanted us the most was the wife of a big Hollywood producer at Columbia. She was Penny Singleton, famous for having made the long series of "Dagwood and Blondie" comedy pictures. But she wanted a movie with a starring role and she wanted a western.

She had visited some friends in the midwest. She told her husband all she could hear on the visit was people raving about a bandleader named Bob Wills. She heard some of our records and saw our pictures. She decided that she was going to have Bob Wills and His Texas Playboys in her movie.

So we went to Hollywood to make *Go West Young Lady*. The male star was Glenn Ford.

He was a nice guy. He would stand around during the breaks and talk with us. He said he really liked our music. He treated us as equals. There wasn't any of that snob stuff.

We did our music on a tape first. Later, when they were filming, you would follow the tape and synchronize the sound with the motions. We surprised Morris Stoloff, the music director, that first day.

He had some regular musicians standing by to play the music score for us. We told him there wasn't any use for

142

him to hire them. He looked apprehensive until we started playing. Then he began smiling and keeping time with the music.

"You boys really surprised me," he said. "I thought I was really going to have some problems. I thought you were just a bunch of . . . well, I hate to say this, but a bunch of country hicks."

We played for Miss Singleton and she sang several numbers. Then we played while Ann Miller sang and danced. Then it came time for several of our country numbers. Bob gave me the chorus on "Liza Jane." I hit it. Mr. Stoloff screamed, "Hold it. Hold it."

I thought he was going to run me off. I just knew I had fouled up badly. But he had some stage hands bring out an old upright piano that had been fixed to sound rinkydink. Then he said, "Now, Mr. Piano Man, let's hear you go."

I went. He loved it.

We finished the movie in about three weeks. We had some time to kill so we went to Ocean View Park. We rode all the rides. Then we went around to some of the concessions. We found a place where a guy was setting up some whiskey bottles on a shelf. He was barking, "Break three of the bottles and you win yourself a dollar."

You were supposed to break the bottles with a sling-shot. You shot round metal objects. It cost you twenty-five cents. Tommy stepped up.

"Let me see that thing," he said.

Fifteen minutes later, Tommy had won over ten dollars. The guy paid him and pulled his canvas down.

"This place is closed. Shut. You boys can leave," he said.

Tommy laughed. He said, "Tell you what, mister, breaking those bottles was a helluva lot easier than shooting those rabbits I used to when I was a kid back on the farm."

"Your family must have eaten a helluva lot of rabbits

143

PLAYBOYS pose for publicity shot with Penny Singleton for "Go West Young Lady" movie.

PENNY SINGLETON, star of the Blondie and Dagwood series, with Bob Wills and His Texas Playboys on the set of *Go West Young Lady* in which they appeared. This was a full-length western shot at Columbia Studio in 1941. From left to right: Leon McAuliffe; Louis Tierney (standing); Eldon Shamblin (left of Al Stricklin); Al Stricklin at the piano; Lew Kemper; Gene Tomlins and Wayne Johnson (behind Bob); "Hoopy" McCray (with trombone); Jamie McIntosh; Don Harlan; Tommy Duncan; Zeb McNally; and Darrel Jones.

the way you handle that thing," growled the man.

Before we returned to Tulsa, we made our recordings. Those songs were "Blue Bonnet Lane," "Bob Wills Stomp," "Li'l Liza Jane," "Please Don't Leave Me," "Cherokee Maiden," "Ride on My Prairie Pinto," "Got a Letter from My Kid Today," "It's All Your Fault," "Goodnight Little Sweetheart," "Dusty Skies," and "My Life's Been a Pleasure."

Members of the band were Bob and Louis Tierney, fiddle; Zeb McNally, sax; Don Harlan, sax and clarinet; Granville King, trumpet; Jamie McIntosh, trumpet; Hoppy McCray, trombone and arranger; Darrel Jones, bass; Eldon Shamblin, standard guitar; Leon McAuliffe, steel guitar; Gene Tomlin, drums; Tommy Duncan, vocals; me, piano; and Lew Kemper, emcee who also sang.

I didn't know it, but this would be my last session with Bob until twenty-two years later. I certainly wasn't thinking about that. I was too full of Hollywood and the sights we had seen when we left for home.

We coasted along with our normal routine the rest of that year. But all of us were reading the newspapers about what was going on in Europe. The news wasn't very good. I remember reading a report from the German chief field marshal, Hermann Goering. He was saying that a decisive blow must be struck in Europe. He had said for this decisive blow, his Fuehrer had mobilized all resources. It sounded scarey.

On Sunday, December 7, 1941, we got the news of Pearl Harbor. It came on our day off.

We all gathered at Cain's on Monday. We had been hearing endless comments and discussions on radio. We had heard the president when he asked Congress to declare war on Japan. We were all shocked and dazed. We were like the rest of America. We didn't know what was going to happen.

President Roosevelt asked for the nation's support. Members of the Texas Playboys responded. Tommy Duncan was one of the first to volunteer for duty.

144

"Fellows, it's been one helluva party for me. I've had some really good times. Things I'll never forget. But, somebody needs me more . . . our country," he told us one day.

The next day he went to the recruiting office and signed up. We all felt sorry for him and we decided to go down and offer him some comfort before he shipped out.

We got down there and asked the burly sergeant where Tommy was. He said, "Your friend is back there in the room to your right. Just go on back."

We figured we'd find Tommy hanging his head in sadness. We even figured he might be kinda red-eyed from some crying. We were wrong. Tommy was back there shooting craps with three other guys. He saw us, grinned and said, "Hang around, gang. I can't quit now. I'm hot."

Patriotism was running high in our country. Some people today just can't comprehend the feeling of the people back then. They were rallying to the flag. They were rallying to America. They wanted to help. They felt it in their gut. It started twisting at them. They had to do something. They had to be in on the great effort. They had to answer the cries of need.

As first one and then another of the band left, I began to get that feeling. I felt like I had to contribute something. I was thirty-three, a widower and had a four-year-old daughter. But, I had to make the pledge.

I went down to the draft board. I told a man I wanted to serve. He said, "We need men desperately. But we wouldn't feel right taking a man like you. What would happen to your daughter if something happened to you?"

It was a tough question to answer. I knew that he was probably right that I shouldn't go into the army. But still, I felt like I could do something to help our country. That's when I made up my mind to quit the band and get a job in a defense plant.

I decided that I should go back to Texas where I had relatives who could help me care for my daughter. After I had made that decision, it took me two weeks to get up

145

enough nerve to tell Bob. Believe me, I was scared.

But, finally, one night after playing a dance at Cain's Academy, I went up to Bob and told him I would like to talk to him a minute. We went to the back of the bandstand. I started talking. I said, "Bob, I've got to do something. It's got hold of me. I've got to try to help our country out. I feel like I should quit the band and go to work in a war plant or do something so I can feel like I am contributing."

Bob pulled that big white hat off. He rubbed his hands over his eyes. When he finally looked up, he had tears in his eyes.

"Kid, ordinarily I would try to talk you out of this. But due to the uncertainties, and the way things are going, perhaps it is just as well," he said.

He stopped and put his hat back on his head. He continued, "Kid, I had just as soon see either of my brothers or any of my folks leave as to see you leave. This is a sad day for me. But, all these days are sad. I just hope and pray that we will all come through this war and get back together afterwards and carry on as before."

He reached out and grabbed my hand in a firm handshake. He continued, "Go, my good friend, and bless you and keep you, and I will never forget you and what you have meant to me these seven years. There will never be another Alton Stricklin."

So I left. I remember driving home. It was a dark night. I was glad. I never liked anyone to see me cry.

Epilogue

SEVERAL OF THE original Playboys gathered at ceremonies to honor Bob twice in 1972. The first time was on his sixty-seventh birthday on March 6. They had a benefit for Bob at the Tarrant County Convention Center in Fort Worth, Texas. More than 7,000 people turned out.

When they finally introduced Bob that night, the crowd went wild. They broke from their chairs and rushed toward the stage. Bob had been wheeled out there in his wheelchair. He had on his big white hat and was holding a long cigar. The crowd strained their fingers upward.

"Let me touch him. Let me touch him. Just one more time," many hollered.

The Bob Wills magic was still alive.

We got together again in April. This time it was at Bob's hometown, the tiny hamlet of Turkey in the Texas Panhandle. Its population is only 600. But, on that day, more than 3,000 people were there. They had come to pay tribute to Bob Wills.

The Texas Playboys got there early. I wandered down the tiny main street, split in two by a large pavement. Stores were on each side. Many were vacant. But the old barbershop where Bob once had cut hair was still open.

BOB WILLS (in wheel chair) at his Birthday Party in San Antonio at Civic Auditorium, 1971.

AL STRICKLIN with Joe Ferguson setting in with Leon McAuliffe and his Cimarron Boys, Panther Hall, Fort Worth, 1971.

Harold Ham, whose father once employed Bob, was there cutting hair. I looked at the old chair that Bob had once used. Harold doesn't use it any more. He has made a shrine out of it.

"It's the least I could do for a man who has done so much for his hometown," said Ham, a short, stocky man.

I walked outside. The West Texas sand had decided to join the celebration. It was skipping in from the farmland that ran right up to the city limits. The farmers needed a rain so they could get their crops in. The growing sandstorm didn't offer much of a promise for a rain.

I got to thinking about how many times Bob and his father and his brothers and sisters had looked at that land. How they had gone out and put their hands in the dry crust and discovered it was too dry to plant. How they had retired to their wooden house and had drug out the fiddle and guitars and played and sang and prayed for a rain.

My mind tumbled backward to the days after World War II. Bob had served a stint in that and then had gone back to entertaining. He had lived in California, Nevada and several other places. Then he and his wife, Betty, a trim and beautiful woman, had moved to Dallas. They had bought a big building at Cadiz and Industrial and spent $45,000 remodeling it. It was called the Bob Wills Ranch House.

It was quite a place. Dallas had never seen anything like it. It had a large bandstand with hookups for radio, television and public address systems. There were hundreds of tables and one of the most unique bars I'd ever seen. It was about thirty feet long and lined completely from end to end with silver dollars.

The Ranch House had a nursery with baby-sitters to care for young children. The walls were lined with pictures of movie stars and western band leaders and messages of congratulations to Bob. It had a stall for Punkin, Bob's famous stallion. He wanted to say hello to the people too.

When I heard about the Ranch House, I was living in Cleburne, Texas. I got up a party of twelve people, made reservations, and we all went there on a Saturday night.

I bragged a lot going up there that night. I related tale after tale about my experiences with the Texas Playboys and Bob Wills. Finally one of the men said, "Hell, man, I'll bet Bob wouldn't even remember you."

"I'll eat your hat if he doesn't," I said.

Our group was amazed at the Ranch House. We had never seen a dance place like it. We made the rounds and then I headed up in front toward the bandstand. I guess I was kinda strutting. Bob saw me.

"Man, look at who I see out there in that crowd. It's Al Stricklin. Get that man up on this bandstand," he said.

I crawled up on the stage and shook everyone's hand. Then Bob said, "Al, how about playing a little number for us."

I began to beat the ivories and I was soaring like a kite being flown on a windy day at the end of 4,000 feet of string. I finally quit and went back to our table. The guy who had doubted Bob's recognizing me, said, "I'll just be goddamned."

I was walking on down the street in Turkey. I nearly bumped into a group of people. I apologized. I started to leave but stopped. I listened to what they were saying. A stoutly built woman in a flowered dress was talking. She said, "It's such a pity about all them strokes and things that have happened to him. I remember him when he was a kid and he was such a dashing young man and was wiry and strong. I just can't imagine it happening to him."

I walked on. The sand was really dancing around the streets now. I got to thinking about when the bad things started happening to Bob. I guess it really started when old Punkin died. That was in 1963.

He was already old and had been retired. One of Bob's good friends, Roy Parnell, had a ranch near Stephenville,

Texas. When Punkin started getting old that's where Bob sent him. That's where the great stallion died. He was buried on a hillside out on the range. Somehow, his death started a series of bad things.

Shortly after that Bob had his first serious heart attack. Many people would have quit and given up. But not Bob Wills. As soon as it was possible, he was playing again. Bob loved to entertain people and see them happy. It was his gospel.

My stroll had led me to a little drugstore in Turkey. It was like the old-fashioned drugstores. Wide shelves and everything from purgatories to aspirin to handmade sodas and malts were sold. There were dozens of people in there. I went in and ordered me some coffee.

Somebody recognized me. They said, "Aren't you Al Stricklin, Bob's old piano player?"

"Well, I won't admit to being old, but I'm Bob's piano player," I replied.

They got to talking about all of the awards Bob had won. My mind began drifting again. I started thinking about some of the many awards Bob had won.

His first really big award was in 1951. He received a plaque from the Western Artists and Disc Jockeys of Southern California for his "everlasting contribution to western music."

There were many more. He was given a life membership in the Cowboy Hall of Fame in Oklahoma City. In 1970, he was presented an award by the All American Country, Folk and Western Club International.

But the big one was the annual Country Music International's honor at its annual Hall of Fame Installation in Nashville in 1968. He was named to the Country Western Hall of Fame, joining such greats as Roy Acuff, Tex Ritter, and Chet Atkins.

That honor was a really big one for Bob. He and Betty figured he had no chance of being nominated for anything. They even talked about not going. But a friend convinced them they should. When the honor was announced, Bob was speechless. He took off his hat and stood there while applause rang out for five minutes.

On May 31, 1969, the beginning of the end started for Bob. He suffered a massive stroke. It actually started the day before when he had been in Austin, Texas, for a big celebration. Bob was there along with Ernest Tubbs and Tex Ritter, all native sons of Texas. They were honored for the contributions they had made to their state.

The next day, Bob awoke feeling dizzy. His hands and arms were numb like he had lain on them. His vision became blurred. By late in the morning, Betty loaded Bob into their car and headed for Tulsa. They had been using a doctor there for many years and Betty felt like that was who should see Bob. The doctor diagnosed a massive stroke. Bob never overcame its effects.

"Hey, fellow, what are you crying about?" It was the voice of a man with a sun etched face. He had grabbed my arm. He was squeezing it. I looked up. I was back in Turkey. I shook my head and thanked him. I left. My coffee cup was still full. But it was cold, like the feeling I had inside of me.

I made my way up to the high school football field. There were several large garden plots around it. The dry, crusting dirt lay in abundance like warped wood chips. The sun was high and hot. But the wind had quit blowing. And, the sand was resting.

They had brought a big truck to the football field. Its bed was going to be the bandstand. Already, there were several thousand people at the bandstand.

We all shook hands and talked to some of the fans. Then we climbed onto the truck bed and began playing our afternoon concert. The crowd was responsive. I wasn't surprised. It always was that way when the Texas Playboys played.

After several numbers, Jesse Ashlock, Sleepy Johnson and Curley Lewis began playing a round of breakdowns on their fiddles. Bob was sitting there in his wheelchair.

Suddenly he got Sleepy's attention. His face had a beam on it. Sleepy bent down. One of Bob's hands, which had been paralyzed by the stroke, was lying in his lap. As Sleepy leaned over, Bob started noting the fiddle with his good hand. Sleepy kept pulling the bow.

It caught us all by surprise. One by one, we looked over at what was going on. The old master was fiddling again. The music was coming from those fingers, that had held plow handles and workhorse reins and many great fiddles. They were turning out music again. We all started crying.

Sleepy kept on pulling the bow. Tears the size of raindrops were running down his cheeks. Then the crowd realized what was happening. They also began crying.

Everyone was crying except one person. That was Bob Wills. He was smiling and fiddling like he had done in the old days. The notes from his tune bounced up into the air and spiralled up into the sunlight. They were trading punches with some of the sand that was in the air from the growing sandstorm. But, Bob's music was winning. There wasn't any doubt about it. You could tell from the looks on the faces of the crowd.

When the song finally ended and Bob quit playing, Leon stood still a minute and looked at Bob. He finally walked back to the mike. He tried to talk. He couldn't. His voice just wouldn't come out. I had never seen him that way.

I don't know how we were able to complete the concert. But we did. The Texas Playboys always gave the audience their money's worth. But that was one day when filling the order came hard.

Afterwards we climbed into our cars and began driving away. Out northeast of Turkey, the road makes a big bend and then dips down into a valley. Then it starts up another hill. When you get to the top, there's a large field.

When I topped the hill, the wind had gotten up again. The sand was kicking up and scatting across the highway.

Out in the middle of the field, a farmer was turning over some of that old dry dirt with his tractor and a plough.

I wondered how many times Bob had faced that sand. I wondered when he was doing that back when he was a youngster if he ever thought that someday that biting dust in his eyes would be replaced by stardom brought on by that great talent of his that made his fiddle music a sweet harmony for millions to enjoy.

I kept driving. The sand was really up now. It was making a steady, biting noise at my car, sounding like someone was hitting it with BBs. It kept reminding me of something but I couldn't quite put my finger on it. Then it hit me. It sounded like the steady tapping of Bob's boot when we were playing and he was keeping time with the music. That's a sound I'll never forget . . . a sound that millions learned to dance to and busted their vocal chords shouting "ah-ha" to in keeping up with the master.

AL STRICKLIN and Floyd Domino in Houston at the Hoffines Pavilion.

"BROTHER AL" with "Miss America, 1976," Phyllis George at the
Celebrity Breakfast in Fort Worth.

AL STRICKLIN at the Exit Inn in Nashville, Tenn. in 1975, setting in with "Asleep at the Wheel."

THE AUTHOR ticklin' the ivories at Napoleon's Pizza in Fort Worth.

"BROTHER AL" hams it up during radio show in Cleburne, 1954.

AL STRICKLIN relaxin' at the piano.

THE AUTHOR "sweatin' out" another country music dance.